S0-ATF-930

Anger in Love

Books by Samuel Southard
Published by The Westminster Press

ANGER IN LOVE
PEOPLE NEED PEOPLE
THE FAMILY AND MENTAL ILLNESS

ANGER IN LOVE

by Samuel Southard

THE WESTMINSTER PRESS · PHILADELPHIA

Copyright © MCMLXXIII The Westminster Press

PUBLISHED BY THE WESTMINSTER PRESS ®
PHILADELPHIA, PENNSYLVANIA

PRINTED IN THE UNITED STATES OF AMERICA

Library of Congress Cataloging in Publication Data

Southard, Samuel.
  Anger in love.

  1. Anger.   2. Marriage counseling.   I. Title.
BF575.A568   616.8'915   73-7997
ISBN 0-664-24975-2

1793360

To

Chaplain L. H. Mayfield
Christ Hospital, Cincinnati, Ohio

Chaplain George Thompson
Hermann Hospital, Houston, Texas

Chaplain Wayne Cook
Methodist Hospital, Lubbock, Texas

for the opportunity of presenting
in clergy and nursing seminars
the ideas that became this book

Contents

Foreword

Anger is so different in the two worlds of my life. In the church it is an emotion that is seldom acknowledged and never to be expressed. A hostile person was automatically unchristian, it was thought.

In a mental health institute, anger is not only expressed, it is often sought after. If a person can work up a "gut feeling" of rage in group therapy, others congratulate him for "really being authentic." Staff members note hostility in colleagues, and expect the feeling to be acknowledged rather than repressed.

If only we could bring these two viewpoints together! The church knows the ethical principles that redeem anger and has taught the careful control that can sublimate a troublesome emotion. The mental health profession knows the depths of anger and the value of expression in an accepting surrounding.

There is no need to decide for one world against the other, but I do think that the accepting view of anger means more to us when we are young and the controlling view is more valuable when we enter adult responsibilities. I am not suggesting the extinction of anger with age. I am asking for consistency. We need authorities who take a stand and can be relied on to be indignant when their policies are subverted. I deplore the weakness of supervisors and managers who vascillate before opposition and never use their rage to protect subordinates against injustice. There is a time to be mad, even when our own relationships are jeopardized. Only a man of principle can "swear to his own hurt" without changing.

Anger is the cutting edge of character. It is the emotion that hardens our resolve to do justice despite opposition. It is indignation that moves into action when those we love are mistreated. It is the strength to stand firm when we might retreat because of continual hostility or resentment from others when we seek to do right and block their attempts to do wrong.

Anger is a necessary but troublesome emotion. Although indignation is essential for character-building in the face of entrenched evil, it is also possible for rage to go astray into selfishness, hostility, or violence. Anger may be smothered and burn in the unconscious until the whole personality is consumed by an unknown complaint against the world.

How are we to know when we have a right to be mad, and how are we going to distinguish this feeling from some related impulses that should be rejected? Anger and justice can be related to each other by the application of general principles to specific circumstances or people. In the following chapters, this will be done in the study of an angry marriage. Two people, in love, are miserable because they are mad. They need to see what they do to each other and what is going on inside them. But how can they express anger and still be in love? They must have found some answers, for now they are happier than they have been in years. Maybe it will turn out the same way for you.

1

Good Reasons to Get Mad

"My wife has been angry for weeks! She is so resentful of me and the kids. It's really boiling up since she started to see Dr. Zalampas." Mr. Park almost smiled as he said this. He seemed to be relieved that conflicts were now coming out under some professional control. At least this is what the psychologist, Mr. James, thought as he looked across the desk at Mr. Park.

Since Mr. James and Dr. Zalampas worked as a psychologist-psychiatrist team in the mental health center, they both knew that Mr. Park was relieved to find help for himself and his wife. It had been eight years since he had first sought professional help. Until now, the resentments of Mrs. Park had been masked as vague physical complaints; also, her husband and children "did not love her." For the last three months she had been in a "blue spell." She seldom spoke to her husband, refused all social engagements, fussed at her three children. Her continual tirades against her youngest boy, age eight, had led her husband to insist that she come with him to the mental health center.

Mr. Park wore a sport shirt, slacks, and casual shoes. He was tan and muscular. Mr. James, the counselor, thought that this man must play golf every day. He smiled readily and did not seem tense or nervous.

How could this active man control his anger and at the same time let his wife express the rage of a lifetime? Mr. James knew that his advice would sound like a contradiction, but it would be the first goal for these interviews. Mr. Park would have to learn how to use his own anger constructively and to understand that his wife was showing something deeper, a hostility that was not directly connected to her daily life with her husband or children.

At least Mr. Park knew that Dr. Zalampas was trying to get at the underlying causes of his wife's rage.

MR. PARK: I tell you, that doctor is trying to get all the hate he can out of Mary. That's what makes her sick. At least that's what the doctor told me several years ago in Rapid City and I believe it. Since Mary has been going to Dr. Zalampas, she has really been stirred up. It's been two months of pure hate. She glares at me in the evening when I come home.

MR. JAMES: So now you want to see if you can take this for a while and what you should do to be of help to your wife at the same time?

MR. PARK: That's right. My minister, who got us to come here, says I can stand just so much. Of course, I can get away for a while. I have a good job and some golf buddies that I enjoy. Then there's the church and my work with the civic club. All those things help to keep me going. But when my wife is really hurting, like she is now, then she hurts me and the children. Maybe I'm doing the wrong things, but once in a while I get angry when she goes too far.

MR. JAMES: Give me an example.

MR. PARK: Well, she never wants to go anywhere. Several nights ago we had the annual dinner for the Kiwanis wives. I've always enjoyed that. I came home early from work to help her with anything so we'd be ready on time. She wasn't dressed. She said she couldn't stand all those fakey people who smiled and laughed and then criticized each other. She began to tear down one of my friends after another. Finally I told her: "Well, you're the worst of the whole lot. You sit around here all day and criticize everybody else and then say *they* are bad." Boy, was I hot! Maybe I shouldn't have been so angry with her when she's sick.

MR. JAMES: Good, good. She needs to know how she can still reach you and she did so. Once in a while she needs a big interpretation from you, so that she'll keep in contact with healthy reality.

MR. PARK: What do you mean, healthy reality?

MR. JAMES: I mean that Dr. Zalampas and I are hoping that you will not just give in to the way your wife sees things. Dr. Zalampas is working on the reasons why she sees things now as she does.

MR. PARK: Sure, sure. The doctor in Rapid City said she had been badly hurt as a child and the real source of her hostility is back there somewhere. I don't go into that—she really gets sensitive when I try to play doctor. Besides, that's what I'm paying you guys for. (*Laughs.*)

MR. JAMES: You're right. Anyway, a healthy reality means that you offer a little different interpretation of events than the one she has. If she gets moody because of some slight from someone you know, don't accept it as a sure sign that people hate her and despise her. That's what she thinks. Give her an alternative explanation, that the person may not have been thinking of her at all when the date for a party was changed, or something like that. There might have been a sick child in the house, or who knows what.

MR. PARK: Well, that's kind of hard to do sometimes. She says I don't know what's going on, that I'm too optimistic, that I'm always looking at the bright side of life.

MR. JAMES: Then you will have to be more realistic—I mean, remind her of other occasions when the friend has gone out of the way to show her concern and kindness. Be as factual as possible.

Mr. Park had been sitting back in the chair a few minutes as he listened to this advice. Now he sat up straight and spoke.

MR. PARK: That's good, but I still wonder if it's right for me to be mad at her.

When Should I Get Mad?

How will Mr. Park know when he is right to be angry? Should he have raised his voice when his wife pushed him too far? Will he always want to control himself when she is coldly hostile? If he must smother indignation, then where can he safely show how he really feels?

We have all asked these questions. They are the common problems of a universal situation. The purpose of this book is to show how this emotion can be used either constructively or destructively.

Anger is judged by its companions. If rage is motivated by envy, jealousy, selfishness, conceit, or impatience, it is destructive. But anger can be constructive when it is a part of love, creative power, justice. These are the virtues that make anger moral.

The chief virtue of anger, which Mr. Park has already expressed, is love. The urge to fight is in him when there is danger to his children, to his wife, or to himself. His marriage is threatened by the behavior of his wife, and his anger lets him know that he still cares and wants to do something. He cannot stand idly by while she commits the injustice of blaming him and the children for injuries she suffered long before they knew and loved her.

Mr. Park is particularly in need of help with his feelings because his wife consistently blocks his attempts to love her. She cannot control her hostility, and he is having a big problem with his anger at her attitude. He said: "When I try to show concern for the kids, she says, 'You're just trying to play up to the children and take them away.' Or when I try to do things for her, she says, 'Well, you really feel guilty, don't you? Running around the house, trying to pick up things and make it up to me.' I tell you, I can't win either way with her!"

Anger always has to be interpreted, for it is ethically neutral. The key question is, For what purpose am I indignant? One of the great moral philosophers, Thomas Aquinas, wrote, "He who is angry or afraid is not praised or blamed, but only he who while in this state behaves either properly or not."

There is no virtue in anger for its own sake, but anger can be a part of virtue. When Mr. Park speaks on behalf of his children, he is displaying the virtues of love and bravery. On the other hand, we would not call him loving or brave if he impatiently yelled at the children or cut down his wife with criticisms of her family.

Since anger can be either good or bad, Mr. Park will have many questions to consider: Should I let my wife know when I get angry? What do I do with my feelings if I am trying to suppress my indignation? Is it right for me as a parent to let the children know how I feel about their mother at times, and what about my anger toward them? Am I supposed to be one way at home and another way at the office? Is this anger a help to myself, to my wife, and to my children? Should I keep it up or push it down?

Mr. Park and his counselor would soon be confused if they did not have some guidelines for decision. Toward what goals are they moving? One goal is to harness anger to basic values in life. Anger is not valuable for its own sake. It is a feeling that expresses our desire for action when some valuable part of our life is threatened.

We evaluate anger by the kind of value that leads to this response. When a person is unforgiving, his anger turns in time to hostility. This is the negative form of anger that we see in Mrs. Park. Anger may also be an expression of the desire for quick recognition through the use of force. This is violence. It is the way of weak egos who have strong muscles. Impatience, selfishness, implacable spirit will turn anger toward sullen hostility or sudden violence.

Love, power, and justice use anger for higher purposes. These are the virtues that call forth and control anger.

In a later chapter we will see how love compels and contains anger. It can be the sign that we care and it can specify the cause of alarm. We rise up to defend that which we cherish. By specifying the cause, we contain the anger. We are aroused at this time, in this place, by this person, for this reason. Our energies are concentrated on the solution of an identified problem. Love focuses our concern upon one hurt without diminishing our ability to see the person against whom our feelings are directed. Mr. and Mrs. Park, for example, may learn how to disagree and even to have some heated arguments without breaking their relationship. This is the function of love.

The couple and their children must learn when to show how they feel. But there is also the difficult question: Should I have been angry at all under these circumstances? The answer to that question comes from an inner power of discrimination. We must decide if a value is to be served by any action at the present time. Will we weaken or strengthen love by attaching it to anger in this case? How will other persons interpret what I feel?

These questions about present decisions are to be resolved by justice. Justice is the control center for the expression of feeling. Shall we or shall we not show how we feel? When shall we express ourselves and in what manner? Mr. Park is continually trying to do justice toward wife, children, and self. He must show respect for Mrs. Park as wife and mother, yet protect the children against unjustified punishment from her. He must learn to sympathize with her frustrations and must know when to tell her directly that she is misguided. She may be committing injustices by blaming him or the children now for some problem that came out of her past. Justice sublimates our emotions. That is, it holds our feelings steady upon one object. We do not explode without control. Instead, we try to keep our feelings under control for the sake of some justifiable goal.

It takes some power to keep us steady in a just decision. If we did not exercise firm control, we would move from sublimation to sentimentality, which is the swaying of the self with every impulse. The problem of Mr. Park is to keep a steady hand on his feelings. There are times when he must speak in a spirit of love and self-control. But he must not be indignant about everything. He must know when to say what is needed. He must be direct and selective about the subjects he raises.

Consistent indignation is a strong virtue. It calls for inner reserve and outward watchfulness. This inner and outward alertness to danger will have two values. On the one hand, we will be slow to speak when a sudden impulse goads us, but, on the other hand, when we see that justice is served by an open response we risk ourselves repeatedly for a specified good. The power of anger is increased by our consistent commitment to a purpose beyond ourselves. This is the strong face of love.

In Chapters 5, 6, and 7, we will see how love, power, and justice provide good reasons to get mad and guide our actions. Before we can begin that specific analysis of anger, we must be sure that it is identified and distinguished from some other reaction to frustration.

What's Different About Anger?

Frustration can be expressed in many forms: anger, hostility, aggression, violence. All these reactions seem at times to be the same, but they are not.

Mr. Park has to make some distinctions between his own

anger and a related feeling in his wife. She is full of hostility. At times this bursts forth in gestures and words that seem angry, but there is a difference. Her emotion always seems to lead back into some deeper area of life. The anger on the surface is only a sign of a stronger disturbance that might boil up in the most unpredictable places.

As Mr. Park put it in one interview with his counselor: "My wife is unpredictable. I never know what she will be like when I come home; and when we are out with people, someone will make a remark that reminds her of something that she doesn't like, and bang! That's the end of the relationship."

Hostility is a chronic condition unrelated to specific events or relationships in the present. It is triggered by symbolic actions. A chance remark uncovers buried feeling. The rage that results is inappropriate to the present moment. Our only explanation is that some event in the past has molded this hostility and kept it just under the surface. There was unrelenting, unspecified rage toward a real but shadowy foe.

Anger is more specific. It is our immediate frustration that an intention is blocked. We can associate our feelings with some desire within ourselves, some word in another, some action by a group. In a healthy person anger is a spontaneous feeling that is recognized and controlled. It is not part of a chronic dispute with the world that signifies hostility.

Mr. Park began to understand some of this as he talked about himself and his wife. But how much did his wife understand? How much did Mr. Park understand her? In Chapter 3 we will discuss the psychological hunger that lies behind much of hostility.

During a heated argument, Mr. Park would sometimes

wonder if his wife was going to throw something. He knew of other wives who had beaten their children or attacked their husbands. He also knew that there were times when he wanted to do something physical about his feelings. "It's a good thing that I have an outdoor job," he said, "or I'd really be tied up in knots."

Some husbands and wives can be angry without becoming violent. Their egos are strong enough to tolerate much frustration. There are others who have had no strong personal relationships. They think a physical attack will win them recognition that has been denied in other ways. Violence is a substitute for the feeling that controls relationships with people.

Respect and self-control are necessary if anger is not to turn into beating or killing. In Chapter 4 we will explore this vacuum in the souls of many men which has led them to fight without reason. They were angry without cause.

Anger may be just as active as violence, but it does not result in hurt to others. One of the values of anger is its impelling force toward action, but the manner must be love. Violence, on the other hand, is action built on hate rather than on love, on fear rather than on concern.

When we see action we often say that a person is aggressive. Sometimes an aggressive person is accused of being angry. Mr. Park could probably be labeled this way, for he was an outdoor man who was continually on the move, but his aggression did not lead to violence and he did not think of himself as angry. Instead, his aggression was a force for life, the power for building and creating in his business. At times it might be the instinct for preservation. We protect what we live for.

Aggression and anger are closely related when we are defending what we value. If the aggression is channeled hate, we see hostility in action. But if it is directed by love, we see acts of courage, sacrifice, and devotion. These were some of the values that Mr. Park hoped to gain as he tried to understand himself and his family. He kept moving ahead through many disappointments because he was full of life and hope. In the next chapter we will discuss this surge of life which can be called aggression.

2

Aggression with Awareness

"I can't *make* my wife love me. That's the big lesson for me in these last eight years. Boy, that was a hard one for me to take! All my life I could get what I wanted by concentrating and putting out the effort, but it doesn't work that way with women, at least not with one like Mary. She just curls up into herself and I can't find her!"

Mr. Park gave a wry grin as he finished speaking. What does that mean? thought Mr. James. Has this man really learned that there are limits to what people will give us because of hard work? Has he made some distinctions between the respect that is earned and the affection that is given freely? Does he know what a threat his zeal for life may be to his wife?

MR. JAMES: I gather that you have always pushed ahead and overcome the opposition.

MR. PARK: That's right. In my business you have to stay one jump ahead of your competitors, and we work our young men hard. They're on the job six days a week and sometimes each day is ten or twelve hours long. We pay them for the overtime, but it's a strain. For me, it's life. I love to get out with a crew and build something.

MR. JAMES: And I gather that this is approved by the people you work with and is satisfying to you?

MR. PARK: Sure, sure, I've made plenty of money and I've

enjoyed spending it. The board of directors have no complaints. Their dividends come in every year. I play hard but I play fair. I play golf with my competitors and we drink together. If they didn't push like I do, I wouldn't respect them. I don't care a thing for a man who quivers like a bowl of jelly when you move in on him.

MR. JAMES: Well, do some people accuse you of being an angry young man?

MR. PARK: Huh? (*Pauses.*) I don't think so. I may get angry with some guy who goofs off, but we straighten it out and then I'm okay. I'm not mad at the world, or anything like that. Of course, I *am* angry sometimes in the house, but I try to keep it cool.

MR. JAMES: That's the anger you feel toward your wife?

MR. PARK: I don't know that it is always anger. Let's just say she ties me up in knots sometimes, and I can't get loose. She used to talk a lot about being defeated. Well, now she's learned to defeat me. That's something I learned that last time we went to see some doctors in Rapid City, but I still can't figure out why she has to take it like she does! Most women would be happy with a husband who really gets out and gets things done. But she accuses me of always trying to push her into doing things she doesn't want to do. What am I supposed to do about that?

How Good Is Aggression?

What is Mrs. Park so mad about? She has an intelligent, ambitious husband!

Mr. Park has the necessary drive to build a better world. He has hope and energy to sustain his family during difficult days. There are few self-doubts in his makeup. Opposition is met with imaginative moves that bring him success. He knows what he wants and how to get it. This is the good part of aggression.

Zest for living motivates creative people. It is the surge of life that is essential for growth and adventure. The self-actualized person is happy with himself and is rewarded by society.

But Mr. Park is not completely happy. Mrs. Park sees his quick movements as "pushing people around." She blames him for making impulsive decisions and for disregarding the risks in some new venture. His aggression can cause him trouble.

People who are unsure of themselves are certain to resent those who are. This is one of the battles in the Park family. The wife is never sure of what she is doing. Uncertainties plague every decision. In her early interviews with Dr. Zalampas she described this inner turmoil: "I just never seem to do things right. I try hard to make the right decision, but something always seems to go wrong. It's always been that way. I just give up. But John [Mr. Park] bulldozes his way ahead! He never has a doubt about what he does. I can't stand him when he keeps reassuring me that everything will be all right! He's so unrealistic! I try and try to tell him how things really are, but he always sees the rosy side of life."

Mrs. Park sighed as she finished this declaration. It seemed for a moment that she was going to cry, but then she began to talk about her husband and the tears dissolved into rage. She cannot stand this secure, confident, fast-moving, and successful husband. He is a reminder of the successes that she has not achieved. His view of life is a continual contradiction of all her reasons for being a failure.

Dr. Zalampas thought: If the husband could know more about the thinking of passive people, he would not contribute so much to his wife's negative opinion of herself. She already thinks she is a failure, and his bright reassurances are a horrible contrast to her self-doubts. If he can stop pushing her so hard, she might feel a little acceptance.

At the present time, Mr. Park can only shake his head at his wife's world. The couple present a contrast. He sees the world as a friendly place in which people can obtain adequate rewards through living and loving. She views the world as an unfriendly place in which each person will do in his neighbor without warning. She must continually consider her strengths and weaknesses so that her defenses will be secure. She is angered by her husband's happiness. What right does he have to sing and smile when there is so much misery in the world and uncertainty in her life?

Until Mr. Park can recognize the reactions of other people to his aggression, it will not do him as much good as he thinks. A little awareness of the feelings of others may help him to moderate his pace and have more compassion upon those who seem inadequate.

Weak people are certainly intimidated by Mr. Park. He "comes on so strong" that they try to get out of his way. If trapped, they agree with him. How could they fight him? Then they frustrate him. First, they try to stay away from him; he does not know what they are doing and what problems they may have to solve. They are always beyond his reach if possible. Secondly, they resent his quick decisions and obvious assurance. They do not understand what he is doing and wonder if he is taking away even the little bit they have. Will he grow stronger while they grow weaker? They dare not oppose him, but they do only the minimum that he requires. Then Mr. Park pushes harder to get what he wants. As Mr. James told him in one interview, he is like a man who steps on the accelerator when he should release the emergency brake. If he could find out why people resist him, he wouldn't have to put so much energy into exhorting them to more effort.

If Mr. Park were more aware of the uncertainties of others, he would think twice before plunging into unknown areas of controversy. He might consider some of the entangling alliances of hostility and guilt that surround many decisions to be made in business and in community life.

Mr. Park created one opportunity to discuss his lack of awareness. In the third interview with Mr. James, Mr. Park used this illustration of the advantages that come to aggressive and decisive men:

MR. PARK: I'll tell you why a man needs to make up his mind and stick with the goals he has in life. Just last week I was ready to sign a fat contract for building materials with the Langdon brothers. They took over the old Whittemore business and kept the old man's name. They seemed to think his name meant something. It must—his son's a big stockholder or something. He's in and out of the office and poked in while I was talking about terms. He must have made some objections after I left, because one of the Langdons called me later to say they would have to have more money before the contract could be signed. Now why would somebody mess around like that? When a man has written up a contract and handed it to me, I think he knows what he wants to do. That's what I told Langdon, and I took my business elsewhere.

MR. JAMES: So what do you think is going on between the Langdons and the son of the founder of that company?

MR. PARK: I don't ask, but it's something real touchy. Come to think of it, my father told me once that the Langdon brothers had really taken old man Whittemore for a ride when he sold out to them. Old man Langdon had been a good friend of John Whittemore, and he must have told the boys off, because they made some kind of settlement through stock with the son. I don't care much about those things, but I guess that lots of people talked around town and made the Langdons real sensitive. They never have been much, you know, and the Whittemores have always been respected. I guess they had to treat the Whittemore family right in order to piggyback on that respect. But me, I could never do business—or live—that way!

MR. JAMES: I detect some contempt for people who do have to live that way. And I guess it shows when you are around them.

MR. PARK: Well, yes, I don't take much trouble to hide my feelings. What about you, what would you think of such devious personalities?

What will the psychologist say? On the one hand, he finds this contractor to be an open, honest man who can make a good decision and stick by it. The world needs more like him. But on the other hand, he is in trouble because he thinks that the whole world should be full of people like him. He has contempt for those who are weak and does not understand those who compromise to keep their position. If a man is not straightforward, honest, and hardworking, Mr. Park has nothing to do with him.

So long as this vigorous contractor rejects the weak, the guilty, and the uncertain part of life, his aggression will tear down people while he builds programs. He must come to terms with passivity in others and with the dependent needs of himself. Then his zest for living can be used to help others as much as he helps himself. But where does a self-assured person begin to see and accept this other side of life?

Stopping Along Life's Way

The best way to get Mr. Park's attention was to show interest in the questions he raised about his wife, Mary. He was puzzled by her behavior and grieved by her lack of affection. He would stop to listen when someone talked about the central frustration in his life.

Mr. James tried this approach:

MR. JAMES: So you want nothing to do with these weak people. They probably think you are pushing them around and don't want much to do with you either. I guess I'm saying more than I have evidence for, but I just think this is probably true, because—

MR. PARK: Yeah, that's what my wife tells me. I mean, she says that I push *her* around.

MR. JAMES: You asked about that in our last interview. You wanted to know what you were supposed to do when she made that accusation. Do you guess that both she and some of these people in business feel the same way about you?

MR. PARK: Well, I don't know about that. I mean, I'm not trying to do her in. You know, she keeps saying that she is defeated. Well, how could it be *me?*

MR. JAMES: Oh? Why not you? Maybe you have some goals for marriage just like you go after a construction job or a big contract. If she can keep up, that's fine. If not, she falls short of the goals that you have set.

MR. PARK: (*Sits up in his chair and grimly faces the psychologist.*) What do you mean goals that I set?

MR. JAMES: (*Leans forward.*) I mean that you decide what is to be done in the family and then try to get her mobilized for that action. I know that it's hard at this time for you to talk over anything with her, but I would like you to think back to the time when you might have discussed your goals together. Was there such a time?

MR. PARK: Well, you really shook me up with that one. Well, I thought we both wanted children. Well, anyway *I* did. (*Smiles.*) There I go again. I guess it was my decision, but then she was so uncertain about herself. She didn't think that she could ever be a good mother. She was scared that things might turn out as they had for her mother. You know, she had a pretty bad childhood. I told her things would be great, just great. Besides, I was making plenty of money and could offer good security. Yes, that's a goal that we shared together.

At least she enjoyed spending the money for a while. But now it doesn't seem to make too much difference. Nothing cheers her up.

MR. JAMES: So you provide the money, the reassurance, the goals, and she is unhappy. Understand why?

MR. PARK: Well, not too much, but maybe I will after Dr. Zalampas begins to see us together. I guess I just want her so much to enjoy life like I do.

Care and Confidence

Is it possible for a "pushy" person like Mr. Park to enjoy life with less aggressive people? Yes, if he can bring care and confidence together. But how is this possible?

1. A person who is *realistic* in his confidence will have goals that can be obtained by reasonable effort. If his sights are high, he will not be diverted by small slights. In other words, he can overlook momentary annoyance because he sees large objectives for the future. These will bring lasting satisfactions. Why alienate a possible contributor to a grand plan by fighting over trifles? Weak, uncertain, or mediocre persons may attach great importance to small material benefits or to symbols of recognition. They may wish to be called by their last names, to be asked that they be allowed a rug or pictures in their office, to wait to see if a supervisor will speak to them first in the corridor or will sit at their table during the coffee break. If Mr. Park should unwittingly frustrate one of these small gains with his employees, he can restore good feelings by apologizing or going out of his way on some future occasion to recognize that individual or group. He might send some pictures into the office of an employee who has an inside room with no windows, or order an air conditioner for the faithful bookkeeper who is now upstairs with only a fan. It will

take little cost or effort on his part, but it will win the loyalty of those who make these decisions on the basis of small items.

2. An aggressive person can plan ahead in such a way that he and others will benefit from his program. He considers the rewards of all the persons who are involved and the price that must be met in overcoming obstacles. If the going will be rough, he can explain this to a crew and thus win their allegiance by his foresight and his pledge of support for what they do. He is always ahead of others, but always encouraging them to follow toward goals that are mutually valuable. So long as the employees are facing ahead, there is little possibility that they will fight among themselves. In contrast, squabbles occur in organizations where goals are uncertain and progress is stagnant. People have time to look around and soon begin to defend their territory against others.

3. Although a confident person takes leadership in family or work, his plans do not make him the center of all development. Others share in the planning and in the profits. There is mutual responsibility and recognition. As Abraham Maslow has noted in *Motivation and Personality,* a self-actualized person is rather objective about himself. He is not overinvested in any one enterprise. He works hard and enjoys living, but can evaluate realistically what he is doing and why. There is a certain ability to laugh at himself. When a project fails or criticism mounts, he can observe his own faults and take corrective action if possible. Whatever the outcome, his ego is not seriously damaged. A self-actualized person is not so totally involved in anything that he will stand or fall with one job, one program, one relationship. He does not demand total commitment either of himself or of others. This prevents serious ego injury to anyone. Successes are not too heady

and failure is not too deep. The confident person can win a few and lose a few without elation or despair. He enjoys what he can and expects others to enjoy their success. When there is failure, he takes it as philosophically for others as he does for himself. This means that his strength is a source of stability on the heights and in the depths of life.

4. The objectivity of confident people will enable them to "roll with the punch." Their ends are clearly in mind, so the means can be adapted to changing circumstances. Realistic remedies can be applied to current failures, so that future success is more likely to occur. The self-actualized person will learn from his mistakes, either through his own observation or through encouraging comments from others. The mistakes do not mean that he is an inadequate person; they only mean that he must benefit from his experience. Instead of wallowing in guilt and despair, a confident person begins to consider how he can do better the next time. Strengths are redistributed and weaknesses are protected or discarded.

Mr. Park mentioned one example of flexibility in his third interview with Mr. James: "You know, I used to chew out any man I thought was lazy. Sometimes I was right, but sometimes I was wrong. Some of my foremen began to chew me out about my quick decision. They said we could not keep good men who were just learning if I was going to embarrass them without hearing the whole story. *I* thought it would brace them up and keep them on their toes. The foremen showed me that I made the young men lose face, so I learned to keep my mouth shut until I learned all the facts. Then, I also had to learn that you can't rip a guy's face off in front of other employees. I learned to take him aside and tell him what I thought in private. This showed respect. I should've learned that from my father, but I didn't. Anyway, people aren't so scared of me now, and we tell each other what we think without me knocking somebody's head off."

5. In time, Mr. Park may achieve a fifth characteristic of confidence, which is a reflective and patient attitude in times of crisis or despair. The most noticeable characteristic of a self-actualized person is his ability to look carefully before he places blame. In fact, the depth of his perspective may go beyond praise or blame. He may speak in a matter-of-fact tone about the constructive or unconstructive attitudes of all persons involved in a family or business wrangle. Everybody learns something of benefit from his observations. He tends to look at problems *with* people rather than *against* them. Since he does not believe that one mistake will do him in, he does not demolish others for one error. He speaks realistically of the mistakes that were made, and encourages his associates to untangle the threads of their relationships with him.

We often wonder how these confident people can patiently work through trying circumstances. They have enough resources to believe that solutions can be found. They do not panic or "sell out" in a frustrating situation. They can act decisively, but with faith for the present and hope for the future. By speaking directly to issues in a spirit of self-control, they handle anger in a constructive manner. It does not explode today or go underground into hostility. What Mr. Park has to say to his foremen, he says face-to-face. They know where they stand with him. He can then go home without such regrets as "I wish I'd told that man what I thought." The sun does not go down on his wrath. He gets anger out of his system directly. Thus he avoids the sins of anger: malice, violence, hostility.

His wife, and many other people, cannot be angry without sin. They store up anger for many days until it has formed a substratum of hostility throughout the body. They hold grudges or lose control in violent acts. These are the twisted and frustrated results of anger that we will consider in the next two chapters.

Achievement Motivation

Mr. Park does not understand why his wife is unhappy, because he has not looked at the roots of aggression in his own life. Now that he has been stopped by her depression, he may begin to measure his attitudes against those of others. He will find that she did not have the reassurances that he enjoyed in childhood. She was not shown how to do things right, but was criticized by her mother for any mistakes. She was continually expected to perform without training. In contrast, Mr. Park described his family: "I had an older brother who would help me with anything. Of course, he sometimes made fun of the way I did things. Not like my father. He would always say, 'Well, let's learn from this mistake.' He wanted us all to do well, but I never felt that he would abandon me if I failed in some way. He might be disgusted or disappointed, but that's all. He'd slap me on the back and say: 'All right, Hard Rock, let's try again.' That was my nickname—Hard Rock. So I kept on trying, and here I am."

Mr. Park certainly should be satisfied with his achievements, but he will not be a wise person until he can see the value of his family for that achievement. They have carefully taught him how to succeed. There was patient instruction and plenty of acceptance; his father and an older brother were adequate models.

When this fortunate younger son has realized the advantages of his background, he may say: "Well, I *am* different. Most people don't have the kind of support and encouragement that I received." When he has stopped to think about this, he will have more understanding of the handicaps of self-doubt and self-blame that plague many people, including his wife. He may begin to understand that they cannot move at his pace. They do not start out with as much confidence, nor do they proceed with his joy in accomplishment.

Mr. Park can see some of the differences in the life of his wife and others; he may then consider how his life could become different from that of his own family. There is already one difference. He and his wife are not getting along as his mother and father did. There may be some other reverses that he does not anticipate. Sickness, betrayal by associates, catastrophe in business, the death of children—all are possibilities. He should pause to reflect that the misfortunes of others might befall him. There may be a time when his resources will be strained beyond limit. There may be periods in his life when his depression will, for a moment, be as deep as his wife's.

But the depression will probably be only for the moment. Mr. Park can pause along life's way to look for a little time at the darker side of life, but his zest for living will soon move him again. If he can understand the way that aggression has developed more useful service through patient and competent parents, he will benefit from this pause. There will be some discrimination between the push for achievement in his own life and the rage and frustration that underlie aggression in the lives of others. For them, anger and aggression go together. They boil up with rage when they cannot accomplish much. The frustrations of today remind them of the deprivation of yesterday.

Deprived people not only will see anger as the result of

frustrated aggression in their own lives but they will also interpret aggression as a sign that someone else is trying to frustrate them. In the past, people "aggressed" them. They were continually the object of ridicule or they were pushed aside by those who were stronger. Those who did the pushing were often angry. The impatience or impulsiveness of a parent would be a continual memory in the child of anger-aggression.

These people, as does Mrs. Park, will interpret aggression as anger. To them, Mr. Park is a man to be feared. If you get in his way, he will be angry and run over you. Mr. Park does not see it that way. He is still a happy adolescent so far as aggression is concerned. He is not angry, because he has not been frustrated—except by his wife. When he has learned how to care for her with understanding, he will have a better control of his own aggression. He will be able to combine care for others with confidence in himself.

3

Hidden Hostility

1793360

"I don't have any confidence in myself anymore. Nothing I do turns out right. All the time I'm defeated. It's just no use. I should love my husband and children better. I used to think that I flew off the handle because I was physically ill, but the doctor in Rapid City persuaded me that my nerves were shot. This was my real trouble. Well, I guess it's just me. There is nothing I can do."

There were sighs and pauses between each sentence as Mrs. Park spoke. She would not look at Dr. Zalampas. Her eyes were on her hands, which tightly clutched a small purse.

Dr. Zalampas also sighed within himself. How could such an attractive woman be in such a miserable condition? Her hair was carefully sculptured over her high forehead and close to her wide-set eyes. She was obviously an intelligent person, but was under great tension. She wore an expensive-looking dress over her well-rounded figure.

But the figure was too erect, the smile too forced, the makeup too heavy. Something was buzzing inside Mrs. Park and she could not smother the signals of distress. For years her body had complained because of the subterranean rage in her soul. Now she seemed to be through with excuses: "It's not just something physical, it's me."

However, Mrs. Park never talked about herself for very long without some reference to her husband. After an initial interview in which she slowly and painfully described her chronic depression, the weekly conversations picked up. The second interview ended with some rousing statements of Mrs. Park's: "You keep asking how my husband takes this. You want to know if anybody else has been a reason for my depression. Well, I'll tell you, *he* has. You'll never meet a more smug, self-satisfied citizen. Nobody shakes him—but he shakes everybody else. You should see that invulnerable smile that he has. It gets bigger every time I complain about something. He's *so cheerful, so helpful.* So help me God, I've had all the help from him I can stand!"

Mrs. Park was up and out of the door before Dr. Zalampas could say more than, "You feel—" That shook him. What if Mrs. Park became guilty over her explosive anger and decided that she was not worthy to continue therapy?

Fortunately, Mr. Park pushed his wife back into therapy for another week. She did feel guilty.

MRS. PARK: I feel so ashamed of myself for talking as I did. I don't know what gets into me. But it seems to be this way all the time now. I scream at the children and I abuse my husband. It's an unpardonable sin. (*Mrs. Park looked as if she would cry, but there were no tears. Her face was drawn down as though a heavy weight pulled every muscle.*)

DR. ZALAMPAS: So you feel guilty because you spoke in anger. Where did you learn that this was a sin?

MRS. PARK: So you know what it's like. (*Sighs.*) You get all tense inside and then you just have to tear up something or somebody. If the doctor in Rapid City had not given me those pills, I don't know what I would have done in the last year or two. (*Now Mrs. Park did shed a few tears.*) I know

I shouldn't hurt those dear children, but there have been times when I've thought some awful thoughts. I just don't know how to love.

DR. ZALAMPAS: Well, how could you know how to love if you were never taught?

MRS. PARK: Huh? Oh—well, I think that my husband tries very hard to love me. (*Sighs.*) I just can't respond like I ought to. I was very happy with him when we were first married, but it's different after you have children. I should know. I've had three. Well, he doesn't know what a woman goes through. He thinks I should still be youthful and responsive. Well, I'm not. I've told him he'd just have to accept me as I am.

DR. ZALAMPAS: And does he?

MRS. PARK: Ha! He's about as accepting as my mother was. Either you turn in a perfect performance or you get nothing at all.

DR. ZALAMPAS: She expected perfection from you?

MRS. PARK: Yes, yes. In everything. You don't show anybody how you feel, you just do as the best people expect. Boy, if all those best people knew what went on in our house. My poor father, he really took a lot. I'd like to be kind to him now, but my mother drove him to an early grave. Of course, he never did stand up to her—or for me.

DR. ZALAMPAS: Yeh? Give me an example.

MRS. PARK: Oh, well. (*Pauses.*) I guess the one that really bothered me was the senior prom. I wanted to buy a new dress. My mother said I could wear the dress that my sister had used three years before that. My father said he'd give me the money, but my mother cut him dead with one of her cold stares and he was paralyzed. I know why my mother wanted me to wear my sister's dress. She thought I was not good enough to have one. I've heard her tell her friends that she was amazed that people thought I was as beautiful as my sister. She never accepted that. My sister was everything to her.

DR. ZALAMPAS: And you were nothing.

MRS. PARK: Right. Right. I remember that one of those doctors in Rapid City asked me why I didn't stand up to her once in a while. How could I? I wasn't anything and she was everything.

DR. ZALAMPAS: And how about the here and now? Are you still nothing?

MRS. PARK: So far as my husband and children are concerned. John could get along quite well without me. The kids are always following him around. I'm no good to them. I just cause them trouble.

DR. ZALAMPAS: Let's be specific. How does your husband make you feel like nothing?

MRS. PARK: Well, if you've got everything, why would you need anything else? He certainly doesn't need me. He does everything well in his business. He's always full of energy. He expects me to be the same way. I'll be dead tired in the evening from fussing with the kids and he'll expect me to be bright and cheerful. If I'm not, he wants me to get dressed, so we can go out to eat and to a show. *He* thinks that will make me feel better. Well, it's just that much more trouble for me. I don't want to go. He can't understand that.

DR. ZALAMPAS: So you are quite irritated because he is always expecting you to be as active and cheerful as he is.

MRS. PARK: Always! If I'm not happy, then he wants to do all kinds of things to make me cheerful. He's always on the move. He can't wait for me to rest or feel better. He's got to do something to get me going right now. I just can't take any more of that.

DR. ZALAMPAS: One way to hold him off is to explode.

MRS. PARK: Say, that's right. (*Pauses.*) That does stop him for a while. But then I feel so confounded guilty about it. I don't know. He means well and yet he makes me so mad. I just burn up with resentment about all the times he's pushed me around.

DR. ZALAMPAS: And somewhere you learned you were not supposed to have any resentment.

MRS. PARK: No, my mother never permitted any feelings to show. I was to do what she said. I guess my father resented some of the things my mother did to him, but he never talked about it and didn't seem to show much. He just withdrew unto himself.

DR. ZALAMPAS: Which you have tried from time to time.

MRS. PARK: I guess so. Isn't that better than exploding and chewing out everybody?

DR. ZALAMPAS: Well, it seems that in the past at least you chewed your own insides. Sometimes you just blow yourself apart. You knock yourself to pieces and then you think that you are no good. (*Mrs. Park nods.*) Personally, I think you would be hurt less by some open explosions. Then we could work some on control. But first, some of this resentment must be expressed to your husband, and we will have to figure out a way for you to do it without feeling so confounded guilty afterward.

After a month of conversations with Mrs. Park, Dr. Zalampas told Mr. James what he thought. Mrs. Park was chronically hungry for affection and assurance. She had been continually put down by her mother and left defenseless by her passive father. Resentment of ill-treatment had to be smothered. The original anger of a child had burned underground for years as rage against the world. In the process Mrs. Park thought more poorly of herself than ever.

Now she had a double handicap. First, she was self-defeating. She would not express herself in time for changes to be made. Then, in frustration she would "blow up." Her husband and children would retreat. She was continually critical of others and of herself.

The second handicap was misperception. The well-meaning efforts of her husband were interpreted by Mrs. Park as confirmation of her hopeless condition. He was taking over because she was inadequate. If he tried to cheer her up, she thought it was hypocrisy. How could anyone be cheerful around her when she knew all the misery of the world? As she slowed down, he took over more and more of the household duties. He appeared to be more and more competent, and she thought there was nothing else left for her to do.

Dr. Zalampas and Mr. James agreed that it was time to work on some specific problems. Mrs. Park needed to specify her anger. Mr. Park needed to know why he was irritating his wife.

In this plan of action, the therapists combined some understanding of past reasons for hostility with present alertness to frustration. There would continue to be some attention to the roots of the problem, but there would also be an expectation of fruitful relationships.

Handling the Hurt

When the couple met with the two therapists the following week, Dr. Zalampas gave a statement of purpose:

DR. ZALAMPAS: We thought it was time to meet together. We may decide that more of these meetings are not good for the present, or we may decide to have these meetings along with the individual therapy. Anyway, Mr. James and I wanted to say some things about what we see to date. We wanted to tell Mrs. Park that we understand how deeply she has been hurt in the past. She knows that a lot of her resentment has been pushed inside and has caused what she calls blue spells. All those old feelings will not go away overnight and we hope that you, Mr. Park, will recognize this and will not try to pull her out of her retreat right away. We think that you have everything going for you in terms of a desire both to help your wife and to keep the family together. Sometimes you irritate your wife with your zeal, and I hope we can talk more about that.

Mrs. Park, we hope that you can speak more specifically to your husband about some of the things that bother you. We want to drain off some of that hostility and keep it from building up again. The best way is for the two of you to talk about your complaints before they build up.

We will need to stay together on this. We will need to talk about the way that you see things. Some of your interpretations might need to be challenged. But we are not going to have any healing until we look openly at some of the hurts.

MR. PARK: Well, you're right about one thing. I've been very pushy with Mary. I'm always trying to see that everything comes out all right. Of course, I do want our family to be happy like it used to be. I just never have understood why she can't take things in her stride and keep on going.

DR. ZALAMPAS: Mrs. Park, I wonder if you would give an example of this?

MRS. PARK: Well, I think John is trying real hard—sometimes too hard. Like the last time we had people in for dinner. It must have been a year ago. John had just insisted that we invite these people over. Well, nothing worked out right. I was determined to have everything ready on time, but Freddie, our youngest child, got hurt while I was busy with the dinner. So I had to stop and take care of him. Then, when I got back to the stove the beans had burned. I had spent *hours* snapping fresh green beans for this dinner. John had told these people from the North about the wonderful fresh vegetables we cook in the South. Well, then sure enough he came in with these people and started to brag about my cooking, and I knew that everything was ruined—just ruined. Then, when he saw that I was unhappy he tried to cheer me up and I couldn't be cheered up and felt worse about that. So that's how it goes every time.

DR. ZALAMPAS: Do you remember that occasion, Mr. Park?

MR. PARK: Well, not as well as Mary does. She seems to remember every bad thing that has happened. I forget a lot of them. But I see what she is saying. I do rush into things and sometimes that makes it worse. I always tell her I'm sorry when things turn out badly—

MRS. PARK: Just telling me doesn't help much after everything is ruined.

MR. PARK: Well, when I see that you are having trouble with something, I just naturally want to help. I don't know what to do. If I pitch in and help, it seems to make things worse. If I don't do anything, then I feel like I haven't been helpful. What am I supposed to do?

MRS. PARK: At least you're asking a question. That's the first time you have admitted that you've ever been confused about anything.

DR. ZALAMPAS: Is it really the first time?

MRS. PARK: Well, he certainly seems to be that way *most* of the time.

DR. ZALAMPAS: I corrected you because an ultimate word will usually destroy your attempts at reconciliation.

MR. PARK: What is an "ultimate word"?

DR. ZALAMPAS: Something like "always," "never," "the very worst," and others like that. There is no way for you to look at a problem together when someone has passed ultimate judgment upon you. All you can do then is defend yourself.

MR. JAMES: I would think, Mr. Park, that you were becoming a little defensive because of what Mrs. Park has just said to you.

MR. PARK: Well, yes, she does cut me down right good sometimes. I don't know what I do then.

MRS. PARK: I'll tell you what you do. You back off and say nothing. You act like a house dog whose foot has just been stepped on. You go around for a couple of days in a daze, and then I get to feeling sorry for you and pay you a little attention. Then you come out in the sunshine again.

As the interview continued, the therapists worked on incidents and interpretations. They continually asked for the specific events that lay behind some feeling from husband or wife. They challenged or modified interpretations given by John or Mary.

When the hour-and-a-half session had ended, Mr. Park seemed a little dazed. Mrs. Park looked like a fighting cock who was preening his feathers after a satisfying victory. Both therapists were glad that there would be some individual as well as group sessions. As Mr. James said later: "Wow, I didn't know she could rake her spurs into him like that. She can really be vicious, and he hardly knows how to defend himself. But I think he will learn."

Dr. Zalampas looked forward hopefully to his next interview with Mrs. Park. Maybe her self-esteem would stay up for a few days.

The Weakness of Remorse

Dr. Zalampas is encouraging Mrs. Park to express some of her buried resentment. He tries to use current frustration as an opening for feeling. He knows that she is often guilty when rage erupts, but he believes she has the ability to gain some control over her hostility. He thinks that in time she will learn to be angry for a good cause.

But there are many persons who do not seem to have the psychological resources of Mrs. Park. She thinks badly of herself, but at least she can feel resentment when put down and can assert her right to better treatment.

A certain amount of self-esteem is necessary to sustain hostility. Without this, a person who is hurt can only accuse himself and say that he deserved ill-treatment. The individual who is this low can only feel temporary irritation. Perhaps at some time in the past he resisted his tormentors and there was a painful reprisal. Then he was more filled with remorse. He was already ashamed of himself and now he has "caused more trouble."

Weak people seem to be more concerned about their hostility toward others than about the hostility of others toward them. These are persons who are easily hurt but who continually worry about "getting along" with others. This was the problem with Robert, a middle-aged man who has suffered deprivation all his life.

Robert's parents died when he was very young. He was brought up by grandparents who punished him when necessary. Although he thought that discipline was very important, Robert regretted the demand of his grandfather that he quit school at age sixteen and go to work. He is now ashamed that he did not finish high school. He was slapped many times by his grandmother and frightened by his grandfather, who drank heavily. But he could not say much against them, since they treated him "all right, considering."

A brief happiness came to Robert in a youthful marriage. But his wife died during a routine operation. A second marriage was hell, according to Robert. The wife drank continuously and nagged him to drink with her. He said that he should not do this, since he had epilepsy and the doctors had forbidden him to drink alcohol. Then she would have a temper tantrum and he would begin to drink, because "I don't like to argue. I'm a peaceable man. I don't like to cause trouble. I'd rather leave and let things blow over." Sometimes he would withdraw from home and drink with a friend on the weekend. Then he would feel guilty because he had spent money that should go for his wife and child.

Drinking finally led to his hospitalization. This seemed

to be a happier time in Robert's life. He helped to organize a chapter of AA. He won several prizes for dancing and skating. He was placed on a work-adjustment program with a local dairy that was close to the hospital. So long as he could live at the hospital and go to work each day at the dairy, he seemed to be content. From time to time he would talk about the divorce, which was pending, from his wife and the possibility of marrying again. But he made no moves toward socializing outside the institution.

In a study of depressed patients in one hospital, Chaplains Russell Davis and Andrew Lester found many similarities to the case that has just been described. The patients had vague, diffuse feelings of failure rather than of repressed guilt for major crimes or sins. They were more deprived than depraved. Most of them had sought out one person for affection. That relationship had been satisfying enough for them to continue a search for some love object all through life. They would do anything to keep peace between them and those on whom they depended. There was a hunger for genuine love that might lead to hostility, but the persons felt so helpless that hostility seems out of the question.

The chaplains suggested from their own work with these patients that little time should be spent on the subject of hostility. Instead of probing the patient, the chaplains tried to share themselves. They did not seek to be "too close too quick," but looked with the patient at various problems in living and in loving. They also sought to be realistic about depression. It was not just a passing mood. The patient was helped to lean on people who could give him some love. If he seemed ashamed of his weakness, he could be reassured that all of us need to depend on others at some time. Furthermore, the patients had a sincere desire to be good and loving people. This could be strengthened by praising their kindness and patience. The object was to move from an ethic of shame to a gracious trust.

The Control of Permissiveness

Depression has usually been related to the introjection of hostility. In some cases, as we have just seen, the individual has been so deprived that he suffers from chronic shame rather than from hostility. These are severely deprived persons. It is more common to meet people who have some ego strength with which to mobilize hostility. They may be depressed because the feelings have been deflected from the real object back into the self. Treatment usually consists of encouragement toward expression of hostility. This can raise problems of several kinds.

Among these are the ones of the chronic complainers who are so hard to get along with that most of us avoid them. This redoubles their complaints that "no one cares for me."

A nursing supervisor found this complaint to be continuous from a middle-aged woman who was back in a medical ward for the fourth time in ten months. Her first admission had been for observation, the second for a hysterectomy, the third and fourth for "complications." The patient, Mrs. Worth, had vague complaints and could tell the internist only that she was "weak and run down."

The visit of the nursing supervisor to Mrs. Worth took place on the second day of Mrs. Worth's latest admission. The patient lay on her side, with a cold towel on her head, breathing steam from a vaporizer. She moaned as the supervisor sat down by her bedside.

MRS. WORTH: Oh, you don't know what I have been through, dear. It's more than anyone can understand.

SUPERVISOR: How is that, Mrs. Worth?

MRS. WORTH: Well, no one *does* understand. You have some very sweet student nurses here, but of course they are students. Dear things, they try so hard, but they just don't know what to do for someone who is as sick as I am.

SUPERVISOR: Perhaps you could tell me what you think we should do for you.

MRS. WORTH: Well, I would think you'd know about that! Of course I know, dear, that you must depend on the doctors for your orders. They don't seem to know what they are doing, either. They have had me in here so many times, and I am no better. Confidentially, I believe that new intern is browbeating your nurses. He is not kind and sweet to them. Oh, we do need kindness and sweetness so much in this world. I wish I had some of it from my husband. But he doesn't come to see me when I am in my misery.

SUPERVISOR: What kind of misery are you in, Mrs. Worth?

MRS. WORTH: I am so lonely and I have been betrayed. My daughter doesn't even live with me now that she is married. You'd think a child would have some consideration for her mother. But she is like so many of these young things, thinking only of herself. Some of your students are that way, I must say. They don't come when I call. They can't make up my bed without wrinkles. They giggle and squeal in the hall. No one can sleep. They don't act with dignity—

SUPERVISOR: Mrs. Worth, our student nurses are well trained and have not been accused of these things by anyone else on this floor.

MRS. WORTH: Of course, of course. No one wants to criticize those dear young things. They are so sweet. I don't want you to tell a one of them that I have told you this. But of course you know what I am going through and I know you'll do all you can to help me.

SUPERVISOR: Please excuse me, Mrs. Worth. I will note on your chart that I have been by to see you.

MRS. WORTH: Oh, thank you so much. And I do hope you will be able to do something about these things that I have mentioned.

As the supervisor marched down the hall, she almost ran into the hospital chaplain. She grabbed him by the arm and led him to the vacant sun parlor. There she exploded with wrath against "that impossible woman for whom we have tried to do everything, everything. She demands ten times as much as anyone else and complains all the time. She runs down everyone to everyone else. She is impossible!"

A student nurse appeared at the door with a message that Mrs. Worth had seen the chaplain go by and wanted to talk with him. The chaplain left the supervisor with this word: "This is as good a time as any to have it out with her."

MRS. WORTH: Oh, Chaplain, I'm so glad you have come by. It means so much for a man of God to visit. My pastor and the other ministers in the community have all been by to see me. I know them all by name. Of course, I have wondered when you were going to call. I guess you didn't know I was here, you must be so busy.

CHAPLAIN: No, Mrs. Worth, I knew you were here.

MRS. WORTH: Oh? Well, I did want to tell you what's going on here, because I know you have the interest of the patients at heart. None of the nurses will come in and talk to me or answer my call. My doctor seems to be so busy and really he doesn't know what to do for me.

CHAPLAIN: What could he do for you, Mrs. Worth?

MRS. WORTH: He could make me stronger so I could carry some of my burdens. (*Pauses.*) You know what a burden it is to live alone. I mean, I have a husband, but he doesn't stay in the house much. And my daughter, she married and now she hardly visits me at all. I prepared a fine apartment for her in our house, but she and her husband wouldn't stay in it. You just don't know what young people are like these days.

CHAPLAIN: I think they like to be independent.

MRS. WORTH: Yes, yes. That's it. You know just what to say. Yes, they don't wish to care for those who are sick and in need. Of course, lots of people are that way now. My pastor has not been by to see me like he should. Can you understand why a man of God would act that way?

CHAPLAIN: I guess he doesn't think you are ready to be healed.

MRS. WORTH: What do you mean?

CHAPLAIN: I mean that you suffer because you are lonely, but you drive people away from you because you are continually criticizing them.

MRS. WORTH: How can you say a thing like that? Who have you been talking to?

CHAPLAIN: I have been talking to you. So far you have criticized everyone who has been in contact with you here in the hospital. How can anyone help you when you are always running them down?

MRS. WORTH: Oh, you misunderstand! I want to get all the help I can. Please believe me. If you suffered as I did, you would need help.

CHAPLAIN: Good. Give my ideas some thought and I'll drop by to see you tomorrow.

MRS. WORTH: Yes, yes. And do pray for me, Chaplain.

The chaplain, nursing supervisor, staff nurses, and student nurses all agreed that Mrs. Worth was neglected. On the first day of her hospitalization, she got much attention because of her flattery and demands. But by the second day she had alienated most of the personnel through her excessive demands and constant criticism. The staff had to ventilate their feelings against her with each other in order to tolerate the patient. Then they had to work with each other to see that someone met her minimum medical and psychological demands. It took continual alertness, for people stayed out of Mrs. Worth's room as long as possible. She was her own worst enemy.

The chaplain was the next target for her criticism. The following day, Mrs. Worth was visibly angry. She compared the chaplain to a son that she had not heard from in many years. The chaplain was haughty and proud and misunderstood all that she said. He had taken the precaution of talking with the attending physician before this confrontation. The physician's advice was: "Go to it." With this encouragement, the chaplain said to Mrs. Worth, "If you talked your son as you are talking to me, I know why he has not returned to see you in years."

Mrs. Worth began to cry and to say that she had been hurt by the people on whom she had depended the most. The chaplain replied that this was probably so, but that it was presumably a mutual responsibility. Was she aware of the way in which she had treated those who should have loved her? Mrs. Worth then told how she had leaned on her grandmother and later on a strong pastor until recent years. Now there was no one to support and counsel her. The chaplain suggested that when Mrs. Worth was discharged from the hospital she come in with her husband to an outpatient counseling service. Mrs. Worth said that she would talk over the idea with her pastor.

Several days later, after Mrs. Worth was discharged, her pastor called to say that she "did not want to go near the hospital again." However, she was asking her pastor why the chaplain had been so rude to her and accused her of criticizing people. The pastor felt that he might be able to pursue this subject with Mrs. Worth if the chaplain at the hospital would talk with him from time to time. "Because," said the pastor, "I can stand only so much of Mrs. Worth and then I have to unload on someone."

The nursing staff were both relieved and frustrated. On the one hand, they were glad that someone had talked straight to Mrs. Worth and that she had left the hospital with fewer demands and accusations than previously. At the same time, there was some concern about the future of this woman. What could the hospital personnel do to help her?

In a staff conference, the nursing supervisor said that things went better during the fourth hospitalization because staff members worked together in openly admitting their resentment of Mrs. Worth and shared the burden of her demands. The chaplain's conversation seemed to have set some limits on Mrs. Worth's behavior. The cooperation of the chaplain and the internist meant that Mrs. Worth could not denounce the chaplain effectively to her doctor. Instead, he had told her that the chaplain's counsel was welcome and needed. As he reported this to the staff, the doctor laughed and said: "Then, she reversed herself and said she never wanted to criticize one of the Lord's anointed. She would be praying for the chaplain and for the doctor."

The staff were annoyed with Mrs. Worth, but they learned to work together so that they could avoid being personally provoked to retaliation or rejection. They had faced the difficult problem of controlling their own anger with a hostile person.

Suppose the staff reaction had been one of fear rather than of anger? This probably would have been the case if the patient was physically strong and known to be violent. This is the most troublesome form of anger in both society and individual relationships. We will consider it in the following chapter.

4

The Vacuum of Violence

"When I got home from one job, she told me to lock up all the kitchen knives. I thought she was crazy, but she didn't act like crazy people do. I mean, she didn't holler and scream and run around. But she did seem real tense and jumpy. She wouldn't tell me why she wanted the knives locked up—at least not right then."

This information came from Mr. Parks during his fifth or sixth interview. He looked puzzled. Mr. James thought that this was the first time his client had really seemed worried.

MR. JAMES: Are you worried that your wife might do something violent?

MR. PARK: Well, I did worry some the next day when I took off on a new job. You see, she couldn't sleep the night before. I tried to tell her I loved her and wanted to show it, but she said she was an awful person and then began to cry. After a while she told me she was afraid she would stick a knife into one of the children. That's why she wanted the knives put away. I told her that she wouldn't do a thing like that, that she was a very good mother, and that I depended on her to take care of the kids while I was away.

Well, I worried a good deal the next day as I was flying to the new job. Mary was pregnant then and I thought she might be pretty upset. When I came back that weekend she was really depressed. That was when I took her up to the clinic in Rapid City. I talked to my minister some about what was going on. He asked if I had put too much on my wife. I answered that I had to be out of town a good deal to build up the business. He said that my wife couldn't take it. She was lonely and she needed my help with the kids, especially when another one was on the way.

MR. JAMES: So what did you do?

MR. PARK: So I learned to change diapers!

MR. JAMES: Huh?

MR. PARK: That's right; we still had one kid in diapers. The preacher told me I should figure out something to do around the house, so I figured that my wife hated to change diapers more than anything else. So I learned to change diapers.

MR. JAMES: And that helped?

MR. PARK: Well, it helped some. And then I got to calling home every night when I was out of town and would talk to her and the kids. Maybe that, along with her therapy, pulled her through—for then.

The Whirlwind of an Empty Soul

Mr. Park had begun to fill up the vacuum that might have been occupied by violence. He probably did not recognize the depth of his wife's despair, but he did sustain her by specific actions. He relieved her of a disagreeable task and he called every night to make up for his absences.

Loneliness was one reason for Mrs. Park's fantasy about knives. She could think of no other alternative to the draining routine of a young housewife. She was in a strange city with no friends. There was nothing but baby talk with the children. Other women might have thought of an alternative, such as leaving for mother or telling the husband exactly how she felt. But Mrs. Park had been restricted in her feelings since childhood. Her mother had said that no emotions should be expressed, especially the negative feelings of fear, anger, or frustration. So Mrs. Park kept everything within.

For Mrs. Park, the vacuum was temporary. But for many other persons, emptiness is a chronic condition. This is the explanation for continual violence by some people. They have a hollow core that is quickly filled with explosive anger. They cannot endure frustration. In a study of violent men, Hans Toch developed the consistent picture of a person who feels that others have contempt for him or lack respect for him. He wants to do something about this. The one thing he can think of is violence. He is dominated by a need to save his self-image and to hurt anybody who seems to threaten it.

Why does a weak person act destructively? Two answers came from the study of Dr. Toch. One is that a violent person assumes that human relations are power-centered one-way affairs. A person who feels threatened must exert all possible energy toward the domination of others. Violence is a desperate effort at self-assertion based upon self-doubt.

A second possibility is that the violent person sees other people as tools designed to serve his needs. By pushing others around, he will gain respect and confidence.

Both of these assumptions are related to some precipitating action by another person. A police officer may speak or act in a way that seems to put down a suspect who then lunges at the officer. One man at a bar may make remarks that seem insulting to the person at his elbow who then starts a fight. The violent person is touchy, and there usually is someone close at hand to touch the chip on his shoulder.

To chronically violent persons a fight seems the shortest route to desired goals. It is the road to recognition when no other way is known toward self-respect.

Who Lacks Control?

A violent man has certain characteristics that distinguish him from a more healthy person who is occasionally provoked to aggression. In *The Vital Balance,* Dr. Karl Menninger mentions five of these. First, the violence is open. Aggressive impulses are not disguised or concealed. There are times when a violent person will openly admit that if he had a gun he would shoot a certain person. When he gets the gun, he does. This naked aggression can be distinguished from the occasional outbursts of a hostile person: "I'll get that S.O.B." The feeling is strong, but is contained within social limits. The result may be harmful and the motivation vicious, but it probably will not result in death or physical injury. Resignations or divorces are more common results.

The lack of social control is a second characteristic of violent men. They disregard custom, flaunt laws, think nothing about regulations. When these transgressions are noted, they usually shrug their shoulders and say that they did not know or care. Sometimes they bring up some stereotype objection to social reality. In one case, a violent prisoner sought to justify his hostility by describing to me the inadequacies of his doctor.

A third characteristic of violent men is an impairment of perception, judgment, and consciousness. This is not always the case, but it is commonly found in those who are under psychiatric treatment. In fact, it was the most common characteristic that psychopaths noted among their fellows in a ward for the "criminally insane." As one told me: "This place is full of nuts. That man killed his wife and doesn't remember it. The guy in the corner was all bloody after he hit his son with an ax. He don't remember nothing, but keeps talking about blood dripping from the ceiling." Violent men may remember what they have done, but often say they were "out of their heads" at the time or that they seemed to be in a dream and then wake up.

The fourth characteristic is remarkable to most people. We usually would expect great remorse after destructive action, but violent men are more relieved than remorseful. The whirlwind of violence has removed some tension from their system. They have done what they can to preserve self-respect. Their justifications for their actions cannot be shaken, because they actually feel better. They may even recount their experiences with much relish. There is a visceral quality about the remarks. As the guard in an institution for delinquents said to me: "I let the boys fight, like prizefighting, every evening. Man, there's nothing like sinking your fist into the pit of another man's stomach."

A fifth characteristic is the ambiguity of episodes. Some persons who are prone to violence will get in any number of fights or continually destroy property. Others are guilty of only one or two major explosions. Before and afterward, they do not seem to have much trouble in ordinary social contacts. These are usually the persons who have tried one intimate relationship in life, and it failed. The result is injury or death to a husband or wife, parent or child. As these persons are incarcerated, they are usually regarded by prison personnel as good workers. The one-time murderers are thereby distinguished from the belligerent prisoners who have a long record of minor assaults. The latter group are hard to work with anywhere.

The Redirection of Anger

Fortunately for the Park family, Mrs. Park was not as empty as the violent men of Dr. Toch's or Dr. Menninger's studies. She had some ego strength and her husband cared for her and took some remedial action.

But the husband was no great hero. In fact, Mr. Park was a big factor in Mrs. Park's desperate thoughts of homicide. He had always thought that his actions had kept her from killing one of the children. Actually, as she told her psychiatrist, "the knife was for him."

MRS. PARK: It took a little time for me to think this out, but now I'm sure that I really wanted to kill John. I might have figured it out back then, but they put me on so much dope that I really couldn't think straight for a while. And then things got better. He seemed to really be concerned, so I felt more ashamed of myself and tried to look and act better.

Dr. Zalampas squirmed uneasily in his chair and thought: Was I right to take her off medication? She's talking more openly about hatred for her husband. Does she have the control to keep from killing him? Dr. Zalampas folded his hands and tried to look calm and concerned.

DR. ZALAMPAS: I gather then that the knife was not really meant for the children.

MRS. PARK: No, no, I love them, as much as I could—or can. They weren't bad children, they just kept me exhausted. I didn't have any help. What I needed was my husband or somebody for a little relief—just someone to talk to or to take care of the kids for a little while, so I could have a nap or a good night's sleep. But he was never there. He was so busy. All of it was supposed to be for us, but I never saw any of the money and I never saw him. I know now that I was angry with him, but I couldn't do anything about it. I wasn't supposed to. My mother had taught me that.

DR. ZALAMPAS: Well, now, where do the kids fit into this business about the knives?

MRS. PARK: Well, they were there and they were annoying me and I got so confused that I thought getting rid of them would give me some peace. Oh, no, that's not quite it. What I really thought was that if I could just once show how I felt, I would feel so much better.

DR. ZALAMPAS: You mean if you could do something violent, then you would be able to get some of that hate out of you?

MRS. PARK: Yes, that's it. But of course I never could. John acted better and began to stay home more. And I'm sure the pills and the talks with the doctors helped carry me through.

DR. ZALAMPAS: Good, good. But I wonder about that hatred for your husband. We talked some about that a few weeks ago. I hope I will not make you feel too guilty if you say something more about it.

MRS. PARK: Oh, yeah. That was the time when the four of us were together. Well, it's a funny thing. About a week later, when the kids were asleep and we were sitting in the den, he just opened up and started talking about himself. He was going to leave town the next day and he seemed kind of sad and lonely. He doesn't like to be away from us now so much. So he said that he needed me very much because he had never known anybody that really needed him. I mean, his parents had been strong people—not like mine—who cared a great deal for him and were happy to have him around, but they could have gotten along okay if he were not at home. In fact, they do. They aren't like my mother, who has to keep after me about everything that's going on.

DR. ZALAMPAS: Your husband was saying that he really needed you?

MRS. PARK: That's right. I wanted to cry and laugh at the same time. It was such a good feeling. He has always been so strong, you know. I don't know why he would need me. But it seemed like he meant it and I was all warm inside.

DR. ZALAMPAS: It feels good to know that you really matter to somebody in the right way.

MRS. PARK: Well, I guess so. I don't see what I do for him, but maybe I slow him down or show some concern for him, or something like that. I really couldn't answer him very much. He just squeezed my hand and blinked a little bit and said he hated to be taking off for a few days. He is getting quite sentimental, you know.

DR. ZALAMPAS: He must really be thinking about some things, like how much you mean to him.

MRS. PARK: (*Shrugs her shoulders.*) Well, it's about time.

It is also time for Mrs. Park to be more specific with her anger. For years she has smothered her resentments or displaced them upon people who could not or would not retaliate. Her original anger was against her mother and this chronic resentment has not yet been resolved. Then her husband became the lightning rod around which her rage vibrated. He was held responsible both for his own errors and for the compounded feelings of a daughter against her rigid mother. But the rigidities of the mother prevented the daughter from telling her husband that she could not accept some of his behavior. Feelings went underground again and emerged as obsessive impulses of violence against the children.

The Most Dangerous Room

As Dr. Zalampas talked with Mrs. Park about her impulses toward violence, he was inwardly worried about the possibilities of homicide. He thought that if this woman knew no alternatives, she might do something desperate. Such a thought might seem inappropriate, for Mrs. Park was a well-controlled person who was married to a husband who had never laid a hand upon her in anger. How could the doctor think that she would slash at her husband with a kitchen knife?

Dr. Zalampas had a right to worry about violence between husbands and wives, for one out of every five murders is of husband or wife. In fact, Dr. Marvin Wolfgang found that a majority of all murder victims are relatives, friends, or acquaintances of the murderer. It is usually not difficult to find the perpetrator of a homicide, because the offender is one with whom the victim had an intimate relationship prior to the slaying.

Women usually kill their husbands in the kitchen. Mrs. Park was certainly in the most appropriate place! The most usual weapon is a butcher knife. Usually the homicide occurs in the heat of an argument.

Although the present problem is with a woman who threatened violence, the more common violence is between males. Killing is usually a masculine activity, and men usually kill men. Homicide occurs away from the home, unless a woman is involved. Then the chance of crime at home rises to 75 percent. Where does it take place? In the bedroom. Violence occurs in the place where there has been the most frustration of love.

The Enemy Within

Mrs. Park is being encouraged to verbalize her anger and to specify the source. As she does this, her therapist talks about guilt. He must keep her hatred within limits that she can accept. If she unleashes much rage, she may conclude that she is a horrible person who must be punished. The punishment may be self-inflicted, e.g., suicide.

Mrs. Park has thought from time to time that she would

turn her anger in upon herself. This is what she was taught as a child. As she said in one interview:

MRS. PARK: I can still hear my mother's reproaches. "You're a bad girl to think this. You should be punished for even dreaming of that." I'd have horrible feelings of guilt. I thought I had hurt everybody. I walked around like I was on eggshells when there was company in the house.

DR. ZALAMPAS: So you thought that you were responsible for everything?

MRS. PARK: Yes, yes. When I was eleven and twelve I used to pray and pray that God would forgive me, but I didn't feel any better.

DR. ZALAMPAS: Was this about the time that you discovered that you were a woman—that is, you began to menstruate?

MRS. PARK: Oh, I never talked about that with my mother, although she gave me several lectures on the subject and said that someday I would be married and would have to put up with the burden of a man wanting me physically. That is about as much as she ever could say. (*Pauses.*) But I started to tell you that I never got any relief from my prayers. Things just seemed to go from bad to worse. I was doing well in school, but my mother never praised me. There just didn't seem to be anything that I could do well.

DR. ZALAMPAS: So you didn't do anything?

MRS. PARK: Well, I did do a silly thing.

DR. ZALAMPAS: What made you think that it was silly?

MRS. PARK: Well, it just was. Anyway I was just a kid then. But it was a very unhappy time. I didn't have anyone to talk to.

Mrs. Park had been talking to Dr. Zalampas for several months when this conversation took place. He wondered why she had brought up the subject of her life as a twelve-year-old. He knew that she needed to talk some about her mother, but he didn't want to push that subject too fast. After all, if she could learn to get along with her husband, she might not need to face up to everything about her mother. She might bear less resentment and guilt if she did talk more about the mother, or she might become more depressed. He wasn't sure.

Several weeks later, Mrs. Park went back to the subject of her childhood. Her mother had just finished a visit to Mrs. Park's new home. (Mr. Park had decided that fresh surroundings were just what his wife needed.)

MRS. PARK: I didn't think that I could stand a visit from my mother after we had just finished moving. Of course, I wasn't as bad as I had thought.

DR. ZALAMPAS: You mean, you had lots of help.

MRS. PARK: (*Pauses.*) No (*thoughtfully*), I mean to the contrary that I had to make more decisions than usual. I guess that something must be happening to John. He did push for us to get into this new house, but he did listen to my arguments about it. At first I didn't want to think about moving. I had the old resentments about him pushing me. Sure enough, that was what he was trying. But when I faced him with it, he backed off and said that it should be a mutual decision. Well, there were some things that I wanted different and the plans that he brought out of a magazine were the ones that I had pointed to sometime ago. Then he didn't push me too much about colors of the wall or arrangement of the furniture. He just asked what kind of help I would want from a decorator and said that he would pay for it. So for once I picked out my own decorator and made some of my own decisions. I was tired after all those decisions, of course, but at least I was doing a few things for myself. In fact, I noticed some things that John didn't about the plans and made some changes. He seemed to like it. (*She seemed to smile.*)

DR. ZALAMPAS: Good, good.

MRS. PARK: Yes, but my mother! She wanted to know why we were spending all this money when we already had a perfectly good house. She didn't like where I put the chest of drawers that she had given us when we moved into our first house. It's a lovely piece and I admired it, but the decorator and I had agreed on where it would go and that just didn't seem to fit in with mother's plan. Anyway, I must have been feeling stronger, because I didn't argue with her, I just let her have her say—just like you have been telling me I ought to do.

DR. ZALAMPAS: But I didn't mean that you should just give in to her.

MRS. PARK: Well, that's what I am telling you. I *didn't* give in to her. I just let her talk. She actually tried to move that chest of drawers by herself, but it was too heavy. So then she told me to have it moved. I just nodded and went out of the room to see about the children. I was angry, of course, but I began to think about something else. She was trying to make me feel guilty just like she had always done as a child. Only this time I wasn't turning it in on myself.

DR. ZALAMPAS: Like you had done when you were twelve years old.

MRS. PARK: Yes, that's right. (*Pauses.*) In fact, that feeling I had as a twelve-year-old was right after we had moved to Kansas City. I didn't know anybody and I was in a strange school. I tried my best to keep up with the other kids. I had had some friends back in my hometown, but it seemed that none of them knew where I was. At least I never heard from any of them for months, and my mother always despised me when I talked about going back home. I would go off to my room and cry. There just wasn't anybody for me. I guess I really hated my mother for moving us to Kansas City. My father really didn't want to go, but she pushed him just like she pushes everybody else.

DR. ZALAMPAS: But I guess you could not admit at the time that you hated her?

MRS. PARK: Oh, dear God, no! That would have been the worst possible sin. She kept telling me how fortunate I was to have such a caring and loving mother. And of course all the people in the church respected her. I think that the minister was scared to death of her. Boy, she could really put her claws into you under a velvet glove. (*Sighs.*) Well, I got to the place that I just couldn't take it, so I took a bottle of sleeping pills.

DR. ZALAMPAS: Oh, so that's it! You were going to do away with yourself!

MRS. PARK: (*Sighs.*) Yes, I guess it was a very silly thing. (*She sighs again and looks at the floor.*) But I thought anyone as evil as I was didn't deserve to live.

DR. ZALAMPAS: Was that all you thought?

MRS. PARK: Huh? (*She looks up.*) Oh, I guess I also thought people would miss me. I mean, I thought my friends back home would read about my death in the newspaper and then they would feel sorry because they hadn't written to me. Then, of course, I would get to go back home. There is a dear little cemetery beside our church at home. (*Mrs. Park begins to cry.*)

DR. ZALAMPAS: And you would have been back home where you were loved by somebody.

MRS. PARK: (*Nods her head and blows her nose.*) Yes, it was just a childish thought, but I was so desperately lonely.

DR. ZALAMPAS: And I believe you also said that you had been made to feel responsible for everything by your mother. That is, you were to feel very guilty if there were any negative thoughts about her.

MRS. PARK: Negative thoughts about my mother? Why, I prayed for her all the time. That's what I was supposed to do. I even prayed that she wouldn't be thrown out of the church when people found out that I had killed myself.

DR. ZALAMPAS: Now what kind of a prayer is that?

MRS. PARK: Oh, it was all silly.

DR. ZALAMPAS: Now, listen, you have called this "silly" long enough. Where did you get the idea that all this was silly and childish?

MRS. PARK: Well, isn't it? (*Doctor shakes his head.*) Well, it certainly isn't *right* for me to do a thing like that.

DR. ZALAMPAS: I didn't say it was right. I just want to find out why you thought that you were so silly.

MRS. PARK: Well, wasn't it silly? (*Looks a little surprised.*)

DR. ZALAMPAS: I don't think so. You were desperately lonely. Most people who think about suicide, think of it after some great loss. In your case, you had lost the only people who had really cared about you. People also think about suicide when there is no other way out. You had tried hard to please your mother and to make friends at school, but nothing seemed to help. Then I guess it is most important of all to think about the way you were turning hate in on yourself. That's what really drives people to kill themselves, I believe. They can't talk about their hostility toward someone whom they are supposed to love. They feel guilty for all those thoughts, and finally they punish themselves.

MRS. PARK: (*Nods her head thoughtfully.*) Yes, I guess you have a good point there. My, I could never have told myself then that I was justified in my feelings about my mother. In fact, I never even dared to think about those feelings. I was so confounded guilty, and oh I did miss my friends so much. For years afterward I would dream of being back home again. It would have been so wonderful. (*Sighs.*)

DR. ZALAMPAS: Well, you're still living through some of that again here. It has been many years, but you still remember how much you longed to be back home. See how strong that feeling is? There's nothing silly about loneliness and grief.

MRS. PARK: Well, since you put it that way, I guess so. It was just my mother insisting that I should never have any of those feelings. My, she would have stared me right down into the floor.

DR. ZALAMPAS: Did she ever do that?

MRS. PARK: Yes, I can remember her withering me with a glance whenever I said that I would like to go home. Sometimes when she would criticize me I would wish that I could run over to a friend's house, where I was safe, but there was no friend to run to. I would think of saying something to her about that, but it was all no use, no use at all.

DR. ZALAMPAS: You were defenseless and there was no place for you to turn.

MRS. PARK: (*Begins to weep.*) No, no place at all.

DR. ZALAMPAS: But now you have found some safer place to hide?

MRS. PARK: John. Marriage was my hiding place. It was so wonderful for a while. I just let him carry me along from one thing to another. But when it came to the responsibility of children, that was too much. I couldn't stand it. He seemed to expect me to be able to be strong and to do anything.

DR. ZALAMPAS: And of course your mother had expected you to be strong and to do anything—like getting along fine in the city after you were grieving for your friends at home?

MRS. PARK: Yes, I guess that's right. And I guess that I have had some pretty strong feelings about my husband for expecting the same thing from me that my mother did.

DR. ZALAMPAS: Yes. Well, now, are you now a twelve-year-old girl?

MRS. PARK: Huh?

DR. ZALAMPAS: I mean, are you still helpless and lonely and overshadowed by some very strong person?

MRS. PARK: (*Shifts in her chair and stares at a picture on the wall.*) Well, I guess not. I guess I *have* acted like a twelve-year-old a lot of times. Yes, that's it. I have just acted like I was still back there in Kansas City. (*She nods to herself reflectively.*)

DR. ZALAMPAS: Since you didn't think that you could do anything, you intensely resented what your husband was pushing you into, just like you had resented your mother? (*Mrs. Park nods.*) Well, maybe I am also pushing you too far.

MRS. PARK: What do you mean?

DR. ZALAMPAS: Well, I am saying that you are not as helpless and lonely as you used to be. Maybe you don't have to act like a homesick twelve-year-old girl anymore.

MRS. PARK: That's putting it rather strongly.

DR. ZALAMPAS: So I *am* pushing you too fast?

MRS. PARK: No, I guess not. (*Faintly smiles.*) I guess I need to be told to shape up once in a while. Not like my mother would. I mean, you know that kind of pushiness. I guess what I have needed is someone who would understand me and still not let me feel so sorry for myself. Yes, that's it. Well, I've been called a lot of bad things in these last twenty years, but this is the first time that I have been called a home-sick twelve-year-old. But I guess that's the way I'm acting.

DR. ZALAMPAS: Now you have me worried. You're beginning to talk yourself back down into another depression. You are going to feel guilty about having been a twelve-year-old for so long.

MRS. PARK: Well, maybe so, but I'm not so sure. I don't like you telling me that I'm that way. I'm not going to be that way! No, I am *not that way*. (*Frowns.*) You talk about my need to express anger. Well, I'm not too happy about what you just said.

DR. ZALAMPAS: Okay, okay, take it easy. I believe what I said. I believe that you have been thinking of yourself as a twelve-year-old for a long time. But I believe that you have some strengths now that you didn't have in the past. You know that it's okay to feel some anger about your mother and that it is justified. You weren't just a silly school girl. You also know that your husband is not pushing you like your mother did and that he's beginning to treat you with some respect. So now when you get angry you don't have to feel guilty and bury it, and you don't have to fly off the handle and become enraged. You're strong enough to tell it like it is and still keep going.

MRS. PARK: (*Seems to calm down during this speech.*) I see what you mean. You are not saying that I am *still* a twelve-year-old. You mean I have been *thinking* I was, while really I was growing up.

DR. ZALAMPAS: Yes, that's exactly what I mean. Now you're beginning to assert yourself as an adult. You're demanding the right to be treated with respect and you are angry with anyone who does not. Like just now, you thought that I was putting you down and you told me so with feeling.

MRS. PARK: Yes, I did.

When this interview was over, Dr. Zalampas was tired but happy. Mrs. Park had openly faced the truth about herself as a child. She had come close to suicide because of the loss of her friends and the continual repression of resentment against her mother. But now her anger was coming to the surface and she was able to recognize some of the reasons for her resentment in the past. But would she now be so angry with her doctor that she would not come back to see him?

5

Surrender to Love

"I'm *not* going back to that doctor. You can see him if you want to. I can handle my own problems from now on, even if he thinks I'm still twelve years old. I don't have to take that from anybody. You can tell him so if you decide that you are going to see him."

As Mrs. Park said this, and much more, her husband felt a great sense of relief. At the time it seemed strange, for he usually was apprehensive when his wife became this angry. In addition, she was rejecting any more professional help. How would she get along without Dr. Zalampas?

On the day after this outburst from his wife, Mr. Park was able to see his counselor, Mr. James.

MR. PARK: I still can't understand why I took her anger so well.

MR. JAMES: Was it directed toward you?

MR. PARK: No, no. (*Pauses.*) Say, that may be it! She was telling *me* about her anger toward *him*. It was kind of an ultimatum, but when I accepted what she said, she seemed reasonable. I mean, she could talk to me about what happened.

MR. JAMES: That's something new, I suppose.

MR. PARK: It sure is. Usually it takes me days to drag something out of her. But, boy, she came right home from that appointment with Dr. Zalampas and really exploded. It was like some of those explosions with the kids. But then maybe it was not. Well, the difference was that she could talk about this one. She said that he called her a twelve-year-old child, but aside from that she didn't make a lot of accusations against him. Instead, she seemed to be saying that she was going to act like a grown-up.

MR. JAMES: And that made you feel better, even though she was angry?

MR. PARK: I guess I felt a lot of things. I was real glad the doc told her that. She sure has been a child, at times. Well, I guess all of us are that way sometimes, but she sure has been. Well, it was good that she heard it from someone whom she respects. At least, I think she respects him. She didn't knock him the way she does most of my friends.

MR. JAMES: So she was hearing some things that you would like to have said to her but wouldn't have been able to make stick?

MR. PARK: Yeah, I guess so. There are some times when I would have liked to tell her, but I didn't see how she would listen. Usually I make things worse if I make accusations when she's mad.

MR. JAMES: But there was something more this time?

MR. PARK: Well, I sort of felt that she was talking things over with me. When I didn't argue with her, which is what you have been teaching me to do—well, she seemed to be talking *with me* for a change. I mean, she didn't put me in the bag of her enemies and bang us around all together. I didn't defend the doctor and I didn't defend her. I just said that anybody would be angry if they had been told they were still a child. Then I asked her what else he had to say. Well, she said that he said she had been homesick lots of times and then she ended up by saying she had been depending too much on me to keep her going.

MR. JAMES: Had she said that to you on some previous occasion?

MR. PARK: Well, not in those words. I could tell that she resented some things that I would do but she wouldn't *say* so.

Anyway, I told her that I must have annoyed her something fierce by grabbing the ball and running with it all the time in the family. She said, yes, and she had wanted to hurt me some to get back at me for what I had done to her. So I said okay, I guess that I had some of that coming.

MR. JAMES: Then what?

MR. PARK: Well, the kids came running in and I asked if she wanted to go out to supper or eat at home. She said that she wanted to just get off somewhere, so I then asked if she wanted it to be the two of us or the kids as well. She said that we should pick a place that the kids liked. Sure enough, we had a real good time that evening.

In this conversation, Mr. Park has demonstrated the power of love in anger. He has begun to affirm and to accept his wife even when she is agitated and resentful. He has respected her feelings even though he has been very anxious for her to have a good relationship with her therapist and to continue conversations with him. His desire to push her as he does everyone else has begun to subside. Concern for his wife is now dominant over his interest in having his own way.

From what her husband says, Mrs. Park is also beginning to contain anger. She specifies the cause of her irritation. She can tell when she was provoked, for what reason, and by what person. Her energies are concentrated on the solution of an identified problem. She does not run out of control with a generalized indictment of a person or unspecified accusations against many people, including her husband.

Love keeps the personal element in anger. We can focus on one hurt without diminishing our ability to see the person who has been hurt. Mr. Park can see his wife as more than a raging woman in one moment of time. He can think of the difference between the present control of feelings and her loss of control in the past. He can also identify with the way she feels right now.

Love preserves relationships that are strained. Mr. Park sees more than the cause of irritation. He sees virtues in his wife and hopes for stronger understanding in the future. He is encouraged that her anger has not gone into the underground reservoir of hostility.

Speaking the Truth in Love

Some of the truth about Mrs. Park has been put into words. She does not like what has been said, but she can express her distaste and still accept the judgment that has been made of her. Now she wants to prove to herself that she is an adult. How can she do this?

One of the first steps toward a solution has come with Mrs. Park's admission that she wanted to hurt her husband. This is the unspoken motivation for much unhappiness in immature marriages. Unresolved disputes become chronic because of frustrations from the past. A difference of opinion is a chance to hurt the partner because of an unforgiven or unforgotten injury. Mrs. Park certainly has a stockpile of injuries from which to draw. She can disguise her attacks by the use of some small incident to build up a big case. Or she may honestly admit her basic feeling, "I just want to hurt you sometimes because of the things you have done to me." Then there can be some negotiation toward a settlement of feelings between husband and wife.

Mr. Park has also taken a step toward reconciliation by the acceptance of his wife's feelings. He knows that she has been hurt by his impulsive direction of everything and that these feelings will not magically disappear when he says, "I'm sorry." He must demonstrate some control if she is going to forgive him.

Can this couple restore their relationship, even though Mrs. Park never saw Dr. Zalampas again? Yes, this is possible because both of the people have learned something about the reasons why their love was blocked in past years. Mrs. Park has admitted to Dr. Zalampas that she transferred to her husband much of the dependency and resentment that she had toward her mother. She has "come clean" concerning some varied and festering memories from the past. If she now resents her husband at times, which she will, it can be a straight relationship. She doesn't have to twist her feelings around some buried memory of another person.

Mr. Park has also learned a few things about himself. He knows some of the ways he is different from his wife. This helps him to control his urge to control. In time he will realize the value of learning what kind of person she is. He has begun to see that there are many people like Mrs. Park in the world and some of them are working for him. If he learns to relate in a more satisfying way to his wife, he will improve relationships with his business associates and employees.

This necessity for self-insight has been stressed by professional counselors who train couples to fight fairly. Dr. George Bach, of the Institute of Group Psychotherapy, believes that there are inevitable tensions between intimate persons. People cannot live together for years and really share their lives without some differences and, occasionally, hostilities. His observation is that people who never fight are not really living with each other. They go through the motions of life without love.

Dr. Bach finds that a year is usually necessary for people to really speak freely and clearly about current frustrations. Twisted memories from the past must be explored. Unconscious explanations for small slights must be uncovered.

But cleansing the wellsprings of love is only part of the work for Mr. and Mrs. Park. They must also concentrate upon the here and now with the insights they have gained from the there and then.

Love is the continual reunion of that which has been estranged. It is the power to keep on caring when there are reasons for disinterest or hate. Mrs. Park must care enough about her husband to forgive his pushiness of the past. She could continue to hold that against him, but then there would be no reunion. In time she may even forgive her mother, but that would be a divine gift. If she is going to enjoy the love of her family, she must also learn to love herself. She must grow beyond the despairing thoughts of a twelve-year-old who tried to kill herself into a grown woman who accepts the appreciation and affection of wholesome people.

How can this couple keep their reunited love? As yet, it is a fragile relationship but they can work out a great deal apart from professional help.

Mrs. Park can stop gunnysacking her complaints. As Mr. Park said in one therapy session, she has a memory for insults and slights that goes back over the years. These must be talked out or discarded. If they are really important, she must tell him at an appropriate time and with some warning. She cannot continue to use inappropriate occasions to blast him, the children, or his associates for insults that everyone else has forgotten. She must substitute immediate anger for chronic hostility.

"Immediate anger" does not mean an impulsive announcement of irritation at any time. There must be some prudence in the expression of irritation. Prudence is a big problem for Mr. Park, and he may have to think as much about this as his wife does. What is the time and place that is best for a discussion of frustrations? The couple must ask, "Can we really talk now?" They began a straightforward conversation when Mrs. Park came home from her last interview with Dr. Zalampas, but the children came in and the conversation was cut off. At least it had begun at a good time. What will be the appropriate occasion for Mr. Park to ask for some of the reasons that his wife has resented him? Can he do this at a time when he is willing to hear what she has to say and she is willing to risk telling him?

Mrs. Park may not need to tell him everything that she resents. He may alter his behavior enough for some problems to disappear. In that case, she can see the change and forgive without hurting him with a memory that is now dead. It would be "childish" for her to say, "Well, you are doing okay now, but you never did in the past." It would be equally inadvisable for Mr. Park to remind his wife at some time that she is no longer acting like a twelve-year-old girl. If he observes that she is more mature, he should enjoy the present without reminders of the past.

Of course, there are some occasions when words must be spoken. Mrs. Park needed to tell exactly how she felt about Dr. Zalampas. Mr. Park respected her for being open to the truth despite her anger. Mrs. Park needed to hear Mr. Park say that anyone would feel anger under such an accusation. It helped her to know that he was sympathetic with her feelings. It is also significant that he offered no excuses for her. He was honest. If he had spoken against the doctor, she would have suspected him of overprotecting her, as he had often done in the past. If he had spoken up for the doctor against her, he would have been suspected of pushing her around. Instead, he said enough to show that he cared, and that was all for the moment.

Words can help or hurt. An immature marriage is characterized by vicious words and attitudes instead of an accurate description of problems. There are innuendos and insults, such as "That's what you'd expect from a member of your family," or "You're the worst person I've ever known," or "Just being in the house with you makes me ill."

The fight is made worse because of the weapons that are used. Afterward, the partners are more hurt or ashamed by the words than by anything else.

The Value of Vulnerability

How can a couple talk in such a way that both can win? The essential decision is the surrender of ourselves to people whom we love. We let down our defenses in their presence. We tell how we feel without excuses. We admit our mistake and are open to their judgment.

This openness to another person is conveyed by phrases as well as gestures, by words as well as by action. When Mrs. Park says, "I feel insulted," she is vulnerable to either acceptance or accusation from her husband. But that is the way of love. In the past, she protected herself by saying, "*You* are an insulting person," or more recently she may have said, "Dr. Zalampas is rude and incompetent."

"I" language will also go a long way toward the re-establishment of love between parent and child. Mr. Park can say, "I get anxious about the way things are going in the family" instead of, "I want you children to know that your mother is sick." Mrs. Park can tell the children that *she* is worried about some of their outside activities or is not able to take some of their games and conversations today. She appeals to the children to understand *her*. In the past she might have thought of this as being selfish. Actually it is realistic and much better than "How many times have I told you—what's the matter with *you?*"

The difference between selfishness and love is also demonstrated by words of correction. Mrs. Park has been put down in the past when her husband said, "I can't understand how anybody can't keep up with things in the house like you." The children were degraded when Mrs. Park would say, "You are the most noisy and ungrateful children that any mother could have." More love will be shown when Mr. Park can state his expectations about housekeeping and allow his wife to state her expectations and her limitations. The children will respond to correction without losing face if mother or father can say: "I can't stand any more noise now. This is all that I can take. Go someplace else."

This kind of language not only prevents fights but it also is vital when conflict develops. In a fair fight we not only admit how we feel but are aware of some of the reasons for this feeling. Mr. Park will probably be somewhat impatient with his wife as with everyone else. As he pushes her to get ready for some engagement, it will help for him to say, "Okay, I know you're irritated, but you also know how impatient I get about things being on time."

Conflicts can be constructive if the partners are open to each other as well as to themselves. That is, it is as important to hear what another person is saying about us as it is to speak the truth about ourselves. A partner should not become our enemy because he has told us the truth.

Instead, we mature in marriage as we allow a partner to make an observation without our being hurt. Instead of retaliation, there is insight. Certainly it will take some time for Mr. and Mrs. Park to come to this, but it is possible. The first sign of this will be his or her ability to reflect on some disagreement and come back later with an interpretation, such as: "I guess I went too far last night and said too much. I didn't really mean to put you down. I thought you were trying to tell me I didn't know anything about disciplining the children. But I guess you were just saying I was too tense and anxious about a twelve-year-old boy going to a party. I guess I am."

In time, a partner can make an observation in love that would have been previously rejected. Mr. Park may anticipate some of the tenseness of his wife and warn her beforehand that she should not entertain unless she is willing to use the maid. In the past, Mrs. Park would always be frugal and try to entertain without help, but something usually went wrong. Mrs. Park can also admit beforehand that she must have some help, either from her husband or from a maid. Mr. Park can slow down his schedule enough to help her at the last minute instead of working at the office until it is almost time for dinner. Someone has to be with the children—why not he? He may be able to understand and correct his behavior when she says: "If you want me to entertain for business reasons, then you must cut back on the business when it is time for dinner. Either come home and help me or arrange your dinners somewhere else." That needs to be said *before* any invitations are issued.

We not only control anger with the truth but we prevent it by looking ahead in love. When our concern is for mutual growth and happiness, we can think of ways in which conflicts can be avoided. In contrast, collisions were inevitable when Mr. Park planned only for the success of his business or Mrs. Park satisfied the conflicts of child-hood by constantly accusing her husband of hurting her and then retreating.

The Parks, like the rest of us, will always have to fight the tendency toward regression. It is not enough for them to have learned why love was blocked in the past. They must also resolve to keep it fresh for the future. This will require some self-development. Inner discipline must go along with loving communication. In this chapter we have concentrated on respect in conversations. Now we must turn to the self-respect that is the long-term antidote for irresponsible anger.

6

The Secret of Sublimation

"You really got where she is. You got her to talk about the problems that have bothered her for a long time. So what if she was angry? It shows that you had touched some real feeling."

Dr. Zalampas was reassured by this speech from his colleague. Not only had he been concerned about Mrs. Park, he was also one down from Mr. James. How was it that a psychologist could maintain a steady relationship with a client, while he, a psychiatrist, was now dropped by his? With a smile he admitted to Mr. James: "Well, you're one up on me. I don't seem to be able to keep up my part of family therapy."

Mr. James enjoyed his little triumph, but saw a bright side in the swift conclusion of Mrs. Park's relationship to her therapist. "Look at it this way. She will now be angry with you. You have uncovered her feelings about her mother and made her more aware of what is going on inside her. When she thinks of that, she will get mad all over again with *you*. The heat will be off the husband. You have done him a favor. He is feeling pretty good about things anyway. I see him only about once a month."

Dr. Zalampas had gotten down to bedrock with Mrs. Park. Now she was able to build up her own character structure on a solid foundation. Although no one was quite sure of the future, there was hope in the knowledge that she had admitted some things about herself without going to pieces. In fact, the last interview had cemented her resolve to develop adult control.

Mrs. Park has touched the secret that sublimates anger: a strong self. If she can develop the inner power of discrimination, she will not be pulled to and fro by conflicting impulses.

Mrs. Park was never a completely helpless person. There was plenty of hostility, but it did not run wild until the crisis of a third childbirth and the later pressures of growing youngsters. She did have some defenses against the eruption of violence. For a long time her feelings were held down and appeared in physical complaints. When they came near the surface again, she was able to tell her husband that she feared homicide. The foundation of her self was shaky, but there was enough good material in her to prevent catastrophe.

Now, with family love and professional help, Mrs. Park can find more satisfactory ways to sublimate anger. She has already begun to feel the effects of love. She has surrendered the security of withdrawal into self-pity and has openly admitted some of her frustrations to her husband. She has begun to learn that problems must be looked at together rather than from the imperious view on one strong person.

Both husband and wife now have the desire to work together, but do they know themselves well enough to avoid the angry scenes that almost disrupted their family?

Knowing and Willing

Complete self-knowledge is not necessary for control of the intimate frustrations of life. We need to know enough to manage ourselves in a tight spot. Mr. Park knows that he has a tendency to push over people, and Mrs. Park knows that she misinterprets slights as complete rejection.

Additional knowledge would be helpful but is not necessary when a couple complement each other and have a relatively stable environment. Dr. Zalampas has to be satisfied with one "depth" interview. He would have been prepared for more lengthy discussions of Mrs. Park's feelings about her father and mother, early associations and present fantasies. Mr. James, who was more oriented to the here and now, was pleased with Mr. Park's brief review of his family background. This led the husband to see the difference between his assumptions about life and those of his wife. So far as the psychologist was concerned, more probing into sibling rivalry or unconscious desires was unnecessary.

Both therapists agreed that the real challenge of the Park family lies in their ability to use what they already know about themselves. The crucial decision is a willingness to act on the basis of new insight. In fact, there might be some virtue in the early termination of these interviews. The Parks are determined to make it on their own. No long-term dependency was developed toward therapists who would listen for hours to conflicts from the past. The couple are now concentrating upon their present and future.

Intelligent motivation will combine love and will. This combination is often called commitment. It is a desire to live by values that are consciously recognized as essential for a good life. More and more the Parks must say to themselves, "What are we willing to live for?"

A Scale of Values

When the Parks, or anyone else, begin to think seriously about their commitment to life, there is a certain uneasiness. We begin to realize that husband and wife are not always committed to the same goals and that there is often self-conflict of goals in one person. There will be some stressful moments as any couple try to affirm what they believe.

As a couple begin to review their values, each partner realizes why he fought the other. We resist when a person comes close to what is really important to us. Mr. Park seemed to know this in one of his last interviews with Mr. James.

MR. PARK: You know, we're getting along better than we have in a long time, but I get an uneasy feeling when I think about some of the things that have separated us. I mean, we're not completely together.

MR. JAMES: Did I ever say that you should be?

MR. PARK: Well, no, but I guess I'd always thought that everything was to be shared in marriage. Anyway, I guess some of my expectations are just not going to be met. I'll have to live with that knowledge.

MR. JAMES: Good, good. That's what I was hoping to hear. There are some differences between the two of you, and you are not crowding her to see everything your way.

MR. PARK: Yeah, well, that is kind of new for me.

MR. JAMES: So, how did you come to decide this?

MR. PARK: Oh, I don't know. Maybe it was just thinking about some of the fights we've had. Maybe I'm just learning more about women. They seem to put some things first that are secondary to me. She is always thinking of what other people are going to say. She wants to know how we're going to look. Maybe that's why she is so sensitive to criticism.

Well, I used to brush all of that aside. I want to know how *we* are getting along. I don't care much about the opinion of others.

MR. JAMES: Wait a minute. Now you say that you used to brush all of that aside? Isn't that why she would be angry and resentful?

MR. PARK: Yeah, yeah. I guess so.

Social acceptance is more of a value to the wife than it is to the husband in this case. In an earlier interview Mr. Park has told of his anger toward his wife because she was always criticizing the children. One reason for his anger is a difference in values. He does not see why she must chide the children for not behaving properly in the eyes of other people. He is more protective of them from other people. At that time, neither parent could understand or discuss their differences. All Mrs. Park could think of was that her husband was excusing the children's unruly behavior. He, in turn, was disgusted because she was thinking more of her good reputation as a mother before friends than she was of her relationship with the children.

Mr. Park may now be able to accept this social value in his wife. Perhaps he is too secure and self-confident. Maybe he should think more of others' opinions. At the same time, Mrs. Park may think better of herself now and be less dependent upon the opinion of others. With more self-confidence, she is not so vulnerable to the neighbors' measurement of her children. She might be a better judge of their character than the neighbors are. When she can say this to herself, the whole family will be happier.

In a study of the hierarchy of values, Professor Milton Rokeach, of Michigan State University, has found that social clashes are often the product of differing values.

The policemen in one city placed "responsibility" high on a value scale and "freedom" rather low. The blacks in their precinct valued "freedom" above all else. Tensions between the two groups were inevitable. When Professor Rokeach brought representatives of these two value systems together, there was a gradual recognition of different goals for living. Neither side asked the other to change, but each side could ask for some respect for differing convictions.

Awareness and acceptance of differing values may contribute to harmony in society. But how can a family mature if the members strive for varying objectives?

Difference Without Disagreement

Who has said that a happy family must agree about everything? The Park family certainly cannot be built on absolute conformity to the same goals. Mr. Park might have wanted this at one time, but soon realized that it was disastrous. The imposition of one set of values upon other members of the family will either submerge resentment or lead to open rebellion.

Of course the Parks, like many of us, have been brought up with the belief that disagreements are bad and conformity is good. The result of such an assumption was a growing depression in Mrs. Park. She felt trapped by a strong husband and a demanding society. The voice of her mother was added to this powerful coalition. If she doesn't agree, then something is supposed to be wrong with her.

Mrs. Park has finally learned that she doesn't have to agree with her mother or anyone else all the time. She can have some opinions for herself without feeling guilty.

This is a direct challenge to her tradition, but it is necessary for her survival as a person.

In time Mr. Park may begin to appreciate these differences without being disagreeable. Why should he be provoked if his wife doesn't jump at his happy suggestions for continual activity? She may do him some good by raising cautions or setting limits.

The recognition of different values will not only reduce the possibility of anger but will also lead through anger to stronger goals for living. For example, Mr. Park will probably make his wife angry when he openly challenges some of her depressive interpretations of the children's behavior. She has many doubts about them and is often distrustful. He is usually glib in an acceptance of their conduct but can be helpful in pointing out alternatives to his wife's despair. On one occasion she assumed that a fight between her daughter and another child at school was going to ostracize the daughter and their other children. He interpreted the fight as a sign that their children could stand up for themselves. His value of self-assurance could be as important to the children as her emphasis upon social acceptance.

If Mr. and Mrs. Park always disagreed, there would be no common basis for the marriage to continue. Their anger would become hopeless frustration and irritation. Fortunately, there were some shared values that cemented the marriage. They did love each other, each in his own way. There was a growing respect for individuality, a virtue that Mrs. Park cherished but had difficulty in acknowledging for her children. There was an emphasis upon fidelity. The couple really wanted to stay together and would not betray each other.

The partners in marriage were also growing in self-acceptance. Now there was a container for love: the self.

Love can be no stronger than that which holds it. As each learned the boundaries between himself and others, there was less cause for irritation. Mutual respect and thoughtfulness began to replace pushiness or pettiness. On the occasions when a person had had too much, his or her anger could be specified. There were definite limits to the patience of the parents and the children.

Without a strong self-concept, neither Mr. Park nor his wife would know their limits. Their feelings of rage would be diffuse and indecisive. Nothing would be accomplished by their anger. There would be generalized accusations and hurt feelings that were magnified by underground hostility.

Instead of experiencing depression and indecision, Mrs. Park is now aware of a new sense of power. She has a desire to act as an adult, to be aware of her feelings, and to express them in a responsible way. She still has some bitter feelings from early days with her parents, but these are no longer connected to present relationships. She has a will to find a better way of life because of what she has learned about herself and about what is expected from her husband. She can consciously suppress some of the problems that formerly led to fussing or fighting.

But just what should Mrs. Park suppress? Now that she and her husband have a will to work together, they must make some decisions about the appropriate occasion for indignation and the time when some inconvenience or irritation should be passed over in peace.

7

The Right Time for Anger

"When should I get mad?" Mr. Park thought about this question many times after his conversations with Mr. James. He knew that his wife was better because she had begun to realize some of her reasons for hostility. She didn't feel as guilty about expressions of irritation as she used to. But, thought Mr. Park, I don't want her saying, "I'm mad about this all day long!" There must be some times when anger is justified and other times when it is not.

The answer to Mr. Park's question is found in the application of *justice*. The word describes our ability to decide how to respond in a specific situation. Justice is often pictured as the figure of a Roman holding scales in balance. What are we balancing? Reality and righteousness. On the one hand, we must know the situation, our own feelings, and something about the way that others will interpret an action. On the other hand, we must have a commitment to do good and oppose evil.

The therapeutic conversations of the Parks have helped them to weigh situations more accurately. Mrs. Park is more realistic because she now sees herself without all the fantasies of a deprived child. Her vision is not perfect, of course, but she has a better chance of understanding the situation as it is. Formerly, she interpreted the present in the light of the past. Mr. Park has a better grasp of reality than in the days of his headlong flight toward success. As he looks about him on the job, or as he sits in his home, he is more aware of some differences between himself and less-confident people. He does not expect everyone to see everything just as he does.

This realism has helped to control the anger of the couple. Mrs. Park does not have to react to her husband and to other authorities as she once did to her overpowering mother. An overload of hostility is not dumped into every frustrating moment of the present day. Mr. Park is more relaxed with people who are uncertain and questioning on the job. He still gets impatient, but he no longer chews a man out for expressing doubts about some project or schedule.

What about the other side of the scale, righteousness? The Parks could decide, like many sophisticated people, that they should no longer get upset about anything. Some people come out of therapy with the bland assumption that they will no longer be troubled by the cares of the world. Some of them seem to succeed. They are not only nonchalant about the continuation of any injustices that they have known from childhood, they also take a bystander position when new attacks are made upon their family, society, or belief system. All judgments are suspended. Every action is accepted.

The Parks, and many others, are not quite ready to settle for this moral nihilism. They still get angry when they observe injustice in themselves or in others. In fact, Mr. Park probably would have not pushed his wife into therapy if he had not sustained indignation about her treatment of the children. This was more than he could take. They were suffering for the wrongs that had been done to their mother long before any of them were born.

If Mr. Park had not resented and finally resisted this, the children might have become as disturbed as their mother.

Sustained indignation is a mark of character. It combines righteous awareness with bravery. We willingly persevere in our objections to evil, despite threats and retaliation.

It is fortunate for the Park family that neither therapist tried to reduce their sense of righteous indignation. Throughout the conversations, both therapists would offer positive approval ("Good, good") or give short lectures on what they expected or enjoyed in another person. The couple knew where they stood with these reliable professional people.

It would have been possible for the Parks to dissolve gradually their sense of justice through ceaseless introspection. Some persons have come out of therapy more confused about moral decisions than they were in their previous state. This problem cannot always be blamed on the therapist, but there are times when the therapeutic process is like a slow drip of acid upon the rock of basic convictions.

Morality

Ethical imperatives are not blasted away in some direct attack. They are worn away by incessant questions and insertions of doubt concerning every decision. The result is a person who can acknowledge everything about himself and others without commitment. He or she knows feelings of hate or fear, but it doesn't seem to matter anymore. Everything is so relative.

Righteousness cannot be suspended in relativity. Although our knowledge is incomplete and our motivation is imperfect, some commitments must be made and some risks taken for what we believe to be right. Dr. Zalampas took such a risk in his last conversation with Mrs. Park. He told her what he thought, and knew that heavy judgment was in his remarks. He paid for this by the temporary loss of professional esteem. His client jilted him. But in the ensuing months, he realized through the reports of Mr. James that Mrs. Park was becoming less angry and resentful. Also, as Mr. James pointed out, much of her primitive hostility would now be transferred to the therapist who had told her what she really had been.

Certainly the decision of Dr. Zalampas was a relative one. If he had thought about it, he might have assigned 60 percent of the success to this direct confrontation, and 40 percent success to the continuation of a less-demanding therapy. He decided that the risk of his personal prestige was secondary. The primary concern was honesty with a client he had come to know well. He was now realistic enough for his judgment to have an impact. *What* the impact would be, he could not exactly foresee.

It is the unforeseen element in justice that always keeps the image of a scale before us. We must balance righteous imperatives against realistic situations. We not only must have some convictions but must make clear judgments about the application.

Calculated Judgments

How nice it would be to have time for neat balancing of decisions! Most of us find that we are angry before we have consciously thought through what is happening. There is no time to decide whether we should or should not get mad. The feeling is already upon us.

But there are some preparations that will make our anger more accurate when it is needed or held in reserve when inappropriate.

The calculations are based on our scale of values—the higher the value, the more relevant the anger; the lower the value, the less likely we are to become enraged. For example, Mr. Park placed a high premium upon a parent's relationship to children. He was annoyed by his wife's nagging at them. But, on the other hand, he was not perturbed by a child's fight in school. The opinions of others were very low on his scale of values.

Conversely, Mrs. Park was agitated by any social criticism of the children or an implied threat to her status. Her anger could be triggered by events that did not move her husband, and vice versa.

Philosophically, the scale of values would have a label of "basic services" on one end and "personal recognition" on the other. The first of these labels is related to the distribution of basic services and rights. We assume that each person should have freedom and resources for life, liberty, and the pursuit of happiness. Where there is some inequality in the distribution of basic rights, there is injustice. We should be angry when people are denied jobs, homes, adequate income, medical care, personal respect.

In the family there are basic rights such as individuality, affection, responsibility. Mrs. Park has a right to be angry when her husband pushes her into major decisions that she does not accept. It was only when he let up on this and respected her decisions about the purchase of a new house that she began to forgive him for the way he had been. One of the main objectives of Dr. Zalampas was to help Mrs. Park to recognize the righteous indignation toward her mother. The mother had smothered the basic privilege of individuality in her daughter. That should anger any healthy person.

But Mrs. Park should not confuse basic justice with proportional justice. That is, there is a difference between rage over some basic right and pique because of some petty annoyance. As Mr. Park has thought to himself, homelife will be miserable if he or his wife gets angry all day about everything. There are enough annoyances for this to happen, but it makes life miserable.

When we distinguish basic justice from proportional justice, the occasions for anger are decreased. Why? Because proportional justice deals with the distribution of honor, recognition, or money. We are usually annoyed when someone gets more than we do. This is not the same as feeling angry about the person who gets nothing. Most quarrels are about personal recognition, "getting our share." They begin in childhood as an older brother gets more of an allowance or a prettier sister gets more attention or clothes. In adult life an employee may be angered because his neighbor is granted a new air conditioner although he himself must listen to the rattle of an old one. In the home a wife may fuss at her husband because her allowance is not equal to that of one of her close friends. How can she win social recognition if she does not have the clothes and cars that others enjoy?

Parents are ceaselessly bedeviled by cries of injustice from their children. Usually these are "proportional" demands. One child wants a better seat, one longs for a better piece of steak, one wants more kisses than the others, etc.

None of these choices calls for anger. No inalienable right is involved. Of course, if prejudice against one employee or marked favoritism of one child should become a pattern of behavior, then we move from "recognition" to "basic rights." But most of our daily indignation is over questions of perception. We *think* that we have been ignored or slighted. Who can be sure? What difference does it really make?

Our self-concept is a gauge of our anger over recognition or honor. A person who enjoys himself and other people will seldom be annoyed by some slight. He is not sensitive about his recognition in society. He has a good idea of who he is, and it is fortified from the past by good relationships with his parents and in the present by significant associates. He knows that his wife loves him whether he gets a corner office with two windows or has to stay in the inner office with nothing but a door. The wife will know that she is valued for her care of the children and her concern for her husband even though she must wear the same dress to two parties. If someone makes an insulting remark about her wardrobe, that tells her more about the ungracious person than it does about herself. Why should she be judged by such small things?

Justice Over Anger

What is the process by which we become more gracious and less grouchy in our personal relationships? We can reduce the possibility of anger under petty annoyance and increase our indignation over basic injustices through the daily practice of three activities: listening, giving, and forgiving.

Listening is the realistic part of justice. It is an awareness of our relationship with others and their relationships with us. If we listen accurately, we will suppress anger sometimes and be accurate with it on other occasions.

Mrs. Park needs much practice in listening in the here

and now. She has been so attuned to the there and then that all the present messages were distorted. Unrelated signals from her husband or children would trigger a surge of hostility from the past. They were in despair because she could not hear them.

This condition changed when Mrs. Park began to recognize what she was hearing from the past and also began to listen to her own feelings in the present. Now that she is more aware of herself, she is able to respond accurately and immediately to the words and attitudes of those who love her and those who do not.

Her husband needs to take off his blinders. He has been seeing her through rose-colored glasses, which he wears most of the time at work, at love, or at play. He will make other people less angry and have fewer occasions to fly off the handle if he will see people as they really are. He can then listen to what they are actually saying and desist from judging them by his standards. Everyone will not be as "healthy-minded" as he is. Can he hear that?

Mr. Park should have an easier time with the second practice of justice, which is giving. He does have the ability to plunge into uncomfortable or dangerous circumstances. He can give his energy on behalf of others. He certainly is aggressive. He also can be angry and stand his ground with his wife when she is is unjust to the children.

Giving combines justice with power. Love impels us into the lives of others. But this must not be an impulsive gift. Listening precedes giving. Classical moralists have always maintained that prudence is the first of the cardinal virtues, because it provides the realistic judgment for application of love, justice, or bravery. Mr. Park may be brave enough, but he has not been prudent. That is why he has made so many people angry, including his wife.

The third force for justice is forgiveness. This is a movement toward other people even when they are irritating. Although injustices led the Parks to be angry with each other, they were taught that some attitudes should carry the possibility of forgiveness. Instead of fighting against each other, they began to fight to stay together. That is, they learned to express their hurt in ways that could lead to reconciliation. Both of their therapists kept asking for specific examples of present problems. The couple was urged to say how love had been transgressed in this moment of time but to say it in a loving way. This was not to be sentimental. They were to speak directly but without denunciation.

Mrs. Park will probably not forgive all the injustices that have been done to her. She was hurt too deeply when she could not defend herself. But at least the chronic rage of childhood has been transferred from husband to therapist. And Mrs. Park now wants to be a mature person. Her desire is to give up the resentments of a twelve-year-old. This will require much forgiveness. Some of this will happen because of changed attitudes and action by her husband. But basically she must make the decision to forgive. If the restoration of loving relationships is more rewarding than the continuation of resentment, then her ability to forgive will grow.

Forgiveness is most possible when we have freely given ourselves to another and then listen accurately both to ourselves and to others. Love reunites those who have been separated by anger, and justice preserves this union.